P9-CLZ-908

RAVENNA
NAZIONALE

GIUSEPPE BOVINI
DIRECTOR
OF THE INSTITUTE OF RAVENNA AND BYZANTIUM ART
OF THE UNIVERSITY OF BOLOGNA

RAVENNA
AN ART CITY

*

EDIZIONI A. LONGO
RAVENNA

The present book is not intended to serve as a guide and itinerary for those who wish to see the sights of Ravenna; it aims also at being a record in which cultured persons may find an account of the principal theories which the numerous scholars who have made a study of Ravenna have put forward with regard to the scenes represented in art and to the chronology of the individual buildings.
But so that this little volume may the better serve as a guide, the buildings have been grouped together according to their nearness to one another without reference to the question of chronology.

The groups, as they should be visited, are as follows:

1) *So-called Mausoleum of Galla Placidia - Church of S. Vitale - National Museum.*

2) *Cathedral - Baptistery of the Cathedral - Archiepiscopal Museum - Archbishop's Chapel - Municipal Picture Gallery (Pinacoteca Civica).*

3) *Church of S. Francesco - Dante's Tomb - Piazza del Popolo (Piazza Maggiore) - Church of St. John the Evangelist - Church of Santo Spirito - Baptistery of the Arians.*

4) *Basilica of S. Apollinare Nuovo - So-called Palace of Theodoric - Ex-Church of St. Clare - Church of S. Maria in Porto (in the city) — Cloister of the Convent of S. Maria in Porto and the Lombardesque Loggetta.*

5) *Buildings outside the city: Mausoleum of Theodoric (less than a mile from the centre of the City) - Basilica of S. Apollinare in Classe (just over 3 miles from the centre of the city).*

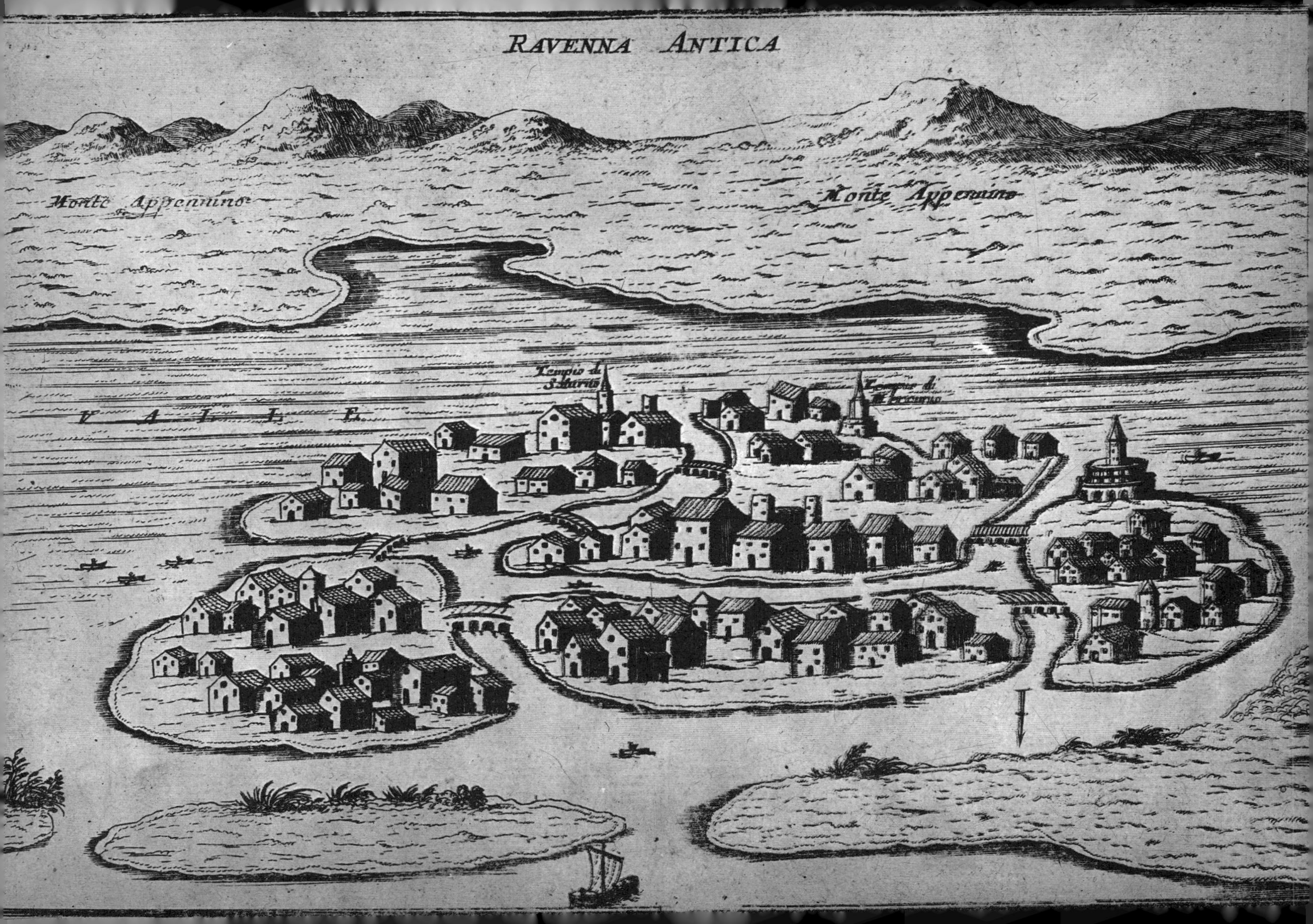
RAVENNA ANTICA
Monte Appennino
Monte Appennino
V A L L E
Tempio di
Tempio di

HISTORICAL SURVEY

Today a wide expanse of well cultivated land encircles Ravenna, but in ancient times the city, which arose upon a group of sand-hills, was washed by the sea and surrounded by marshes. The group of small islands on which the early centre of the city was built was, however, not entirely isolated, for, north and south, it was connected with that chain of dunes which extended to the delta of the river Po on one side, and on the other to the environs of Cervia.

This long chain of sand-dunes at those times formed a barrier against the sea, but with the passing of the centuries, and the accumulation of alluvial deposits brought down by the various branches of the Po, a new crescent of dunes, marking the limit of the foreshore grew up further eastward, starting from Classe and extending northward.

During the Middle Ages and the centuries that followed the low-lying areas were gradually filled up, so that the sea receded more and more, and the seashore is now nearly 4½ miles from the city.

* * *

The early history of Ravenna is lost in the mists of time. Dioniges of Halicarnassus says that the city was founded seven generations before the Trojan War, but we cannot really be sure of this, nor do we know anything of the earliest inhabitants, though Strabo considers that they were of Hellenic descent and had come from Thessaly.

In historic times the city was perhaps inhabited, or rather occupied, for a short period by the Etruscans. This might be deduced not only from the fact that Strabo states that the Thessalonians had to abandon the city as a result of Etruscan attacks, and that they called in the Umbrians before returning to their homes, but more especially from the fact that the suffix *-enna* seems to be typically Etruscan.

Further evidence of the temporary presence of Etruscans in the city might be assumed from the circumstance that some objects undoubtedly of Etruscan make have been found in Ravenna, for example, some small votive bronzes and a fine statuette of a warrior with an Etruscan inscription, belonging perhaps to the 6th century B.C., now preserved in the Museum of Antiquities at Leyden. But it is obvious that such evidence has no definite value, consisting as it does in small portable objects, for these articles may have been used for purposes of exchange, or may have been imported.

In any case the supposition that Ravenna was once inhabited by Etruscans finds no confirmation in historical tradition, which does, however, lay some stress upon the Umbrians, who, as is well known, pushed their way in historical times from Rimini to the banks of the Po.

We do not know exactly when Rome took possession of the city. It is however certain that after the conquest of the Po Valley by the Romans, Ravenna — which had long been a flourishing centre of commerce — was a strategic bulwark of great importance because of its extraordinary geographical position which made it almost impregnable, for it was on one side separated from the inland regions by the marshes, which constituted an excellent defence, while being at the same time in immediate contact with the open sea whence it could easily receive reinforcements and supplies.

It is quite possible that Ravenna's first strong urge to maritime development was due to Marius, for Plutarch tells us that the people of Ravenna erected a marble statue of him in his honour. In any case it seems certain that the first Roman fleet to appear at Ravenna was that of Metellus, Sulla's Legate, who disembarked there in 82 B.C.

Two documents of the end of the 12th century mention also a port of Caius Julius Caesar; but it is obvious that the absence of any earlier evidence does not justify (as Torre has rightly observed) any definite statement or conjecture of any kind on this matter. Yet it is probable that Caesar, who chose Ravenna as his headquarters while treating with the Senate, had, for military reasons, actually carried out some work at the port.

The great development and extension of the port was the work of the Emperor Augustus, who, the better to defend the Adriatic and the seas of the near East, decided to make it the base of a pretorian fleet consisting—so Dion Cassius tells us—of 250 ships.

Thus about 2½ miles to the south-east of Ravenna arose the Port of Classe, whose vast basin was hollowed out at the very place where the most recently formed range of sand-dunes had become separated from the more ancient chain along the shore.

But the work carried out in Ravenna by the founder of the Empire was not limited to the construction of a great military port. He planned a wide canal which should unite it with the southern branch of the river Po. This was the *Fossa Augusti* mentioned by several writers. Before reaching Ravenna it seems to have divided into two branches; the one surrounded the city walls the better to assure defence, the other flowed through the midst of the city thus assisting commercial activity.

In the Augustan era commerce was mainly by water, for Strabo says that in his days the city—where the houses were built upon piles—was intersected by many water-ways regularly swept by the tides which washed out the muddy pools and so kept the air pure. Thus at that time Ravenna, consisting as it did of various islands linked together by numerous bridges, must have presented an altogether remarkable appearance.

Some idea of it—even if not quite corresponding to the truth—may be derived from a graphic reconstruction attempted towards the end of the 17th century by the noted cosmographer of Ravenna, M. V. Coronelli, who, in another design, based especially on information left us by the Arian Bishop Jordanes, tried to show the neighbouring communities of Caesarea and Classe which had developed enormously as a result of having become the permanent station of the great Roman naval fleet.

From that time too Ravenna became familiar with the activities of the shipyards; there is certain proof of this in a funeral pillar (*stele*) to *the faber navalis* i.e. the carpenter of the fleet, Publius Longidienus, who had caused himself to be shown upon in the act of working with an axe near an unfinished ship. While the city was growing in size as a result of the increasing population, it was, at the same time, being adorned with fine sculptures. There is the splendid example of the relief to be seen in the National Museum, showing the members of the Julius-Claudian family.

Like other ancient cities Ravenna had a quadrangular perimeter, only the north-east side deviated somewhat from the regularity of the usual plan because of the two water-ways all along that side. It is probable also that the nature of the ground did not permit the exact orientation of the *cardo* and the *decumanus* with regard to the four cardinal points. In fact, the two main arteries of the city of Ravenna show an inclination of 45°, one running in the direction SW-NE and the other SE-NW. It is thus not possible to decide with certainty which represented the *cardo* and which the *decumanus*. But as the latter was almost always the wider and more important, it is likely enough that in Ravenna it ran SW-NE for a distance of about 490 yards, i.e. from the *Porta Aurea* to *the Pons Augustus* (Via Salara).

This being the state of affairs, the *cardo* must have been on the SE-NW axis and must have had at its extremities those two gates which at a later time were called respectively *Porta Salustra and Porta,* or rather *Posterula Latronum.* They opened in the city wall which was built, or at least restored, by the Emperor Claudius in the first year of his reign, 43 A.D.

The *Porta Aurea,* on the contrary, certainly owes its origin to Claudius, for an inscription (of which today a few fragments remain) mentions Tiberius Claudius. This gate, which had two openings, was flanked by two round towers. In fact it is shown thus on the mediaeval seal of the city, and in drawings left by some Renaissance architects, for example those of Palladio and Sangallo. The two round towers were thrown down by the Venetians at the end of the 15th century and the gate itself was demolished in 1582 merely to supply building material.

Not far from the Porta Aurea stood the Temple of Apollo and the Amphitheatre, but nothing remains of these, nor yet of the Circus and the Capitol, of which the latter stood near the present church of St. Dominic.

At the beginning of the 2nd century the Emperor Trajan provided the city with an aqueduct, for Ravenna, as we learn from Martial, was without drinking water; nor can we be surprised at this when we consider the character of the ground and the nearness of the sea.

So water from the Apennines was brought from the region of Teodorano to Ravenna closely following the Ronco, and when the course of this river was diverted, a few piles and arches of the ancient aqueduct were found in its bed not far from the church of S. Bartolomeo in Longana, in the year 1735.

As it grew in importance and in the number of its inhabitants Ravenna grew rapidly in size even before the 2nd century A.D. Buildings began to arise outside the *oppidum* as the old municipal centre was called, in the region which was later called *Regio Caesarum.*

But a still greater expansion took place at the beginning of the 5th century when the Emperor Honorius made Ravenna the

Capital of the Empire of the West, in place of Milan. The city then soon lost the appearance of a provincial town and assumed the dignity and grandeur of an imperial residence.

Thus, in the new parts which were added to the inhabited area, arose magnificent public buildings and superb churches, the interiors of which were covered with splendid mosaics; such, for example, were the great Ursian Basilica with its five naves and adjoining Baptistery, the Church of Santa Croce and the so-called Mausoleum of Galla Placidia, the Church of St. John the Evangelist, and the church then dedicated to the Apostles, but now to St. Francis.

At the same time the city walls were also extended as a result of the work first of Honorius and Valentinian III, and later by command of Odoacre and Theodoric. With the entrance of Odoacre into Ravenna, and the death of his brother Paul, uncle of Romulus Augustulus, in the pine wood of Classe in 476, the history of the Roman Empire of the West comes to an end. Odoacre was the first of the barbarians to bear the title of King in Italy.

But towards the last decade of the 5th century, preceded by his fame as a conqueror after victories won in battle on the banks of the Isonzo, at Verona, and on the Adda, Theodoric appeared in the neighbourhood of Ravenna at the head of a mighty host of Ostrogoths. After a siege of almost three years, Theodoric, on March 5th, 493, compelled Odoacre—by this time definitely cut off from all possibility of obtaining reinforcements and supplies—to consent to negotiation. It was promised that his life would be spared, and he was given hope that he might retain part of his authority. But ten days later he was accused of treachery and slain in the Laureto Palace, together with his brother, his wife, and later his son.

Theodoric assumed the title of *Dominus*, and later of *Rex*, and—as even Procopius assures us—was a wise and enlightened sovereign. He gave a great impulse to building, undertook extensive work for reclaiming land from the surrounding marshes, and restored Trajan's aqueduct; in fact, some leaden *fistulae* or pipes for the conduct of water found in 1938, bear in relief an inscription which reads: *D(omi)n(us) Rex Theodoricus civitati reddidit.*

Among the great buildings erected by Theodoric must be mentioned his residence, the *Palatium*, and some idea of its exterior appearance—even if only partial—is given by the mosaic showing it at the beginning of the right wall of S. Apollinare Nuovo, but its ground plan is known to us as a result of the excavation carried out by Ghirardini in the early part of this century.

An Arian, and the head of an Arian people, Theodoric wished his subjects to have their own churches. Thus arose the *Anastasis Gothorum*, today the Church of Santo Spirito, which served as a Cathedral, and was near the Arian Baptistery. Beside his Palace Theodoric then erected that stupendous Basilica originally dedicated to the Saviour, today called S. Apollinare Nuovo.

In these churches officiated the Arian Bishops, who, following the teaching of Arius, maintained the heretical doctrine (already condemned by the Council of Nicea in 325 and later by the Council of Costantinople in 381) according to which only God the Father is «*not begotten*», while Christ the Logos is begotten, and he, being different from God, is God by adoption, and not by nature.

In Ravenna there was no violent clash between Arians and Catholics; but some serious conflicts did take place towards the end of Theodoric's reign, for the Sovereign, not satisfied with the results of Pope John's mission (524-525) to the Emperor Justinus in the East and his efforts to obtain favours advantageous to the Arians, kept the Pope a prisoner, and when he died in 526 (little more than three months before Theodoric) he was considered a martyr—*victima Christi.*

In May 540 Belisarius, Justinian's General, succeeded by means of a stratagem in entering Ravenna where the Goths were resisting under the command of Vitiges. Thus the city passed into the hand of the Byzantines, and in 554 became the seat of the Prefecture of Italy. Shortly after Justinian issued an edict granting to the Catholics all the real estate belonging to the Arians. The

Baptistery was transformed into the Church of S. Maria, and the Church of the Saviour was «reconciled» and dedicated to St. Martin, the Bishop of Tours who had so strenuously opposed the heretics. The principles of St. Basil held by the Catholic Church were vigorously affirmed, and one can catch as it were an echo of this reaffirmation in these words written in the book held by Christ in the mosaic that covered the apse of S. Michele in Africisco (now in the Berlin State Museum) which run: *Ego et Pater unum sumus* (I and the Father are One).

A few decades later—as a result of the struggles with the Longobards—power passed into the hands of military governors called Exarchs, who may be almost regarded as Viceroys considering that upon them depended, as Andrea-Agnello—the 9th century historian, author of the «Liber Pontificalis Ecclesiae Ravennatis»—writes, the *regnum et principatum omnis Italiae* (the kingdom and principality of all Italy). In Ravenna the Exarchs, who held civil powers as well as military, established a real court of their own modelled on that of the Emperors.

Just at first the Byzantines brought back into the city all the pomp and ostentation of oriental life, and beautified their buildings with marbles from Proconnesos and mosaics executed by artists trained perhaps at Byzantium.

Sculpture, which had already in the previous century produced works which, for the wide spacing of the figures, was different both from the iconographic point of view and from that of style, from Italic and Gallic sculpture, now takes on a new aspect; one perceives in parapets and capitals contrasts of light and shade determined by the alternation of mass and space; in panels and altar-fronts, in pulpits and in the «pulvini» surmounting capitals, sculpture now adopts a decorative system which finds its typical mode of expression in scantiness of relief and an increased flatness of modelling.

But this splendid artistic impulse lasted only a short time, partly because the great port of Classe, being no longer the station of the fleet, was neglected and fell into disrepair, and lost its original efficiency, becoming in great part silted up. In fact, Jordanes, who was writing about the middle of the 6th century, tells us that where once the ancient port had been he saw not masts with sails but trees bearing fine fruit (*quod aliquando portus fuerit, spatiosissimus hortus ostendit arboribus plenus, verum de quibus non pendent vela sed poma*).

In consequence trade and commerce declined and the city, ill governed for almost two centuries by the Exarchs and then for a brief period about the middle of the 8th century by the Longobards and the Franks, was reduced to the end of its strength, and the efforts of the Archbishops to make the Church of Ravenna independent of Rome, were not enough to maintain the dignity and power of the city.

During the epoch of the Ottos the Archbishops became great feudatories of the Empire, and the city seemed to recover something of its former life.

Thus arose the Comune, among the very earliest in Italy, and it came a *Studio* or University, and a School of Legal Practice (*Ars notaria*). But power soon fell into the hands of the great families, sometimes Guelf, at others Ghibelline, who carried on their feud, till, in the 13th and 14th centuries, the Da Polenta family gained the upper hand and became rulers of the city. Among the members of this family we may make especial mention of Guido Novello who generously offered hospitality to Dante Alighieri, who had been exiled from Florence and died at Ravenna on September 13th, 1321.

From the beginning of the 15th century Ravenna was under the jurisdiction of the Venetian Republic which exercised direct rule from 1441 to 1509, in which year it passed by treaty to the Church. Three years afterwards the city, defended by the armies of the Holy League, was closely besieged by Louis XII, King of France, who took it by storm and sacked it with fire and sword (April 12th, 1512).

A long period of obscurity followed, and with the French Revolution Ravenna even lost its rank as Capital of Romagna, an honour which was transferred to Forlì.

After being returned to the Church in 1815, it was the seat of the Legation till 1859, and in the following year it was definitely united to the Kingdom of Italy.

The so-called Mausoleum of Galla Placidia

THE SO-CALLED MAUSOLEUM OF GALLA PLACIDIA

This is one of Ravenna's most ancient monuments, and in spite of its small size, one of the most impressive. It is generally believed that it was built by Galla Placidia to serve as her mausoleum, and that the Empress was in fact buried there (Ricci). But historical critics (Gerola and Cecchelli), after a careful examination of ancient sources, do not share this opinion, not merely because Andrea-Agnello, appealing to tradition, casts doubt on the matter, but above all because it is certain that Galla Placidia died in Rome on November 27th, 450. It is thus much more likely that the Empress was buried in the Rotunda of St. Petronilla adjoining the Basilica of St. Peter in the Vatican which was used as a mausoleum by the family of Theodosius. We know in fact that a few months before her death Galla Placidia had had the body of Theodosius II interred there after having had it brought back from Constantinople.

No ancient source credits Galla Placidia with having erected this little building, yet, considering the fact that it was originally grafted on to the narthex of the neighbouring Church of Santa Croce—a church which was with certainty built by this Empress—it is held that this pious sovereign did indeed order its erection.

The edifice, entirely built in large bricks, is in the form of a cross measuring about 40 ft. by 33 ft., and at the point where the arms cross it is surmounted by a small square tower which protects the semispherical cupola seen in the interior.

Probably it was intended to be a mausoleum, but it must soon have become an oratory—one of the many in which we know Ravenna to have been rich in early Christian times—nor is there any difficulty in believing that it was dedicated to St. Laurence, since the lunette to be seen at the further end of the axis of the chapel contains a figure in mosaic of St. Laurence hastening eagerly towards his coming martyrdom.

Perhaps the notion that the building was the tomb of Galla Placidia is due to the fact that a number of sarcophagi were placed within it, one of them being considered to be that of the Empress. But they were not there originally; the first mention of them goes back only to the early years of the 14th century, to the period when Rinaldo da Concorreggio was Bishop.

The little oratory as it is at present has sunk into the ground about 4½ ft., and this subsidence has considerably modified its original aspect, for it now appears to be much too low.

With the exception of the façade, all the sides are adorned with uprights which rest upon a skirting (now below the surface of the ground and so no longer visible) and form arches above, thus breaking the monotony of the wall. The oratory is lit by 14 small windows, the lowest ones having the form of loopholes with embrasures within. In 1908 the window spaces were filled with slabs of alabaster presented by king Victor Emanuel III.

The façade, once covered with marble, was isolated in 1602 when the monks of S. Vitale built the new front of the church of Santa Croce which was placed somewhat further back after the front with its porch was demolished.

If the exterior of the little oratory is very simple and modest, the interior is extremely rich and sumptuous. Indeed it reveals

Interior of the Mausoleum of Galla Placidia

such luxuriance of decoration as veritably to astonish the visitor. An atmosphere dim and subdued, but at the same time, especially on bright sunny days, rendered warm and colourful by the golden light which filters in through the alabaster windows, reigns within the chapel, the upper part of which is completely covered with mosaics, while the lower part has a wide band (almost all restored) of slabs of yellow marble from Siena; the slabs were once of the marble called «giallo antico», as is proved by a few fragments still in their original position.

The wide expanse of the mosaic decoration, which is everywhere very well preserved, has as background for its figures a subdued deep blue colour which often shows modulations in tones of whitish grey, golden and pale blue, together with some sober tints of red, yellow and green. The range of colour is thus so delicately varied and shows such a harmonious accord that we are quite justified today in accepting the judgement given in the 15th century by Ambrogio Traversari who declared he had never seen mosaic so refined and so full of grace («Musivum nusquam neque tenius, neque elegantius inspeximus»).

The **Lunette** to be seen **on the further wall** shows a personage clad in white bearing on his shoulder a wide cross while his left hand holds an open book upon which we see writing worked in tiny squares separated one from another; evidently is the Hebrew Scriptures. This personage advances towards the centre of the composition where we see a grating with flames beneath it. On the left side is a small cabinet with open doors showing two shelves on which rest four books; on each of these we read in Latin the name of one of the Evangelists, the books therefore are the four Gospels.

This simple scene has been differently interpreted, for the attempt to identify the personage carrying the book and the cross has given rise to various theories. One theory is that he is a saint hastening to cast a heretical book into flames (A. Venturi). Another (Bottini-Massa) considers the figure in white to be

Mausoleo di Galla Placidia: Lunetta raffigurante il Buon Pastore (V sec.)
Mausoleo di Galla Placidia: Lunette with the Good Shepherd (5th cent.)

Detail of the mosaics of the vaulting

The so-called Mausoleum of Galla Placidia: the sarcophagus called that of Constantius III

the Angel announcing the Final Judgment. Other have thought he represents Christ coming to judge the living and the dead, and holding a book in which—according to a tradition widely held in the 5th century—are recorded the sins and the merits of men (Filippini). This latter theory has recently been taken up again by Seston, a French scholar, who considers that the flames seen in the middle of the composition are lapping the brass grating mentioned in Exodus XXVII vv. 4-5 as being placed beneath the altar of burnt offering upon which perhaps the sinners were to be immolated. Much more obvious, and therefore more acceptable, is the explanation of those who see in the figure the Roman martyr *S. Laurence* (De Rossi, Garrucci, Ricci, Duetschke, Cecchelli, Grabar). In fact, this personage carries the attributes proper to the order of deacons to which St. Laurence belonged i.e. the processional cross and the Book of Psalms, and he has near him what is undoubtedly a gridiron, the instrument of torture proper to him alone. Indeed, considering the determined step with which the saint advances one might conclude that the famous Roman deacon, so much venerated in ancient times, is here shown hurrying towards the fire, or (to use an expression common in ancient stories of the saints) he hastens towards martyrdom—*festinat ad martyrium.*

There is no doubt therefore that the cabinet containing the Gospels appears in the scene as the symbol of the Faith which St. Laurence did not hesitate to give his life.

The mosaic which covers like a soft mantle the barrel vaulting of that arm of the building where this lunette is to be seen, is of highly ornamental character. Upon a dark blue back-ground are many small circles, many stars and many strange flowers. The same design is to be found on the barrel-vaulting of the other arm lying along the same axis. But here, in the distribution of the various elements of the composition, there is a wider and more restful air. In all ancient Occidental art we find no decorative design resembling this; an ornamentation fairly close to it might be recognised only in a Coptic stuff of the 6th or 7th century in the Egyptian section of the Berlin State Museum, but this stuff was unfortunately destroyed in a fire a few years ago.

The small semispherical **cupola** which marks the point where the four arms of the cruciform building meet, is enlivened by the gleam of more than 800 gold stars which, in ever dimishing circles, surround a *Latin cross* in gold at the top. These stars too shine forth from a dark blue back-ground intended to look like the sky at night. From them seems to emanate a glow which would appear to derive, not so much from the interplay of reflexions, as from the intrinsic nature of the stars themselves.

Lower down, near the four spandrels which support the cupola, stand out all in gold above thin clouds of various hues, the *Symbols of the Evangelists*, the Lion of St. Mark, the Eagle of St. John, the Bull of St. Luke and the Angel of St. Matthew.

It is to be noticed how the Cross that shines has its long arm turned towards the east and not to the main axis of the chapel. This is due to the fact that in ancient times sacred buildings generally had the apse towards the east; but here, as the oratory was grafted on to the narthex of the Church of Santa Croce, the architect was unable to give his building the orientation required by liturgical rule, and the decorator thought that, for his part, he could in intent remedy this by giving the Cross in the centre of the starry vaulting the correct orientation.

The high drum supporting the cupola has four **large lunettes** in each of which there is a rectangular window. The mosaicist had to adapt himself to this exigency, and for this reason he placed beside each of the windows two tall male figures. Thus there are eight of them, and each one is wearing a purple-bordered tunic and a cloak adorned with letters. Some are bearded, others not. All, even those of youthful appearance, are in grave and dignified attitudes; with the right arm extended upward they make a gesture of acclamation which Nordström connects with the Cross of the cupola. Above their heads curve wide canopies each in the form of a shell, finished, at the top of the lunette, with a motif of birds' heads and three festoons of pearls.

These personages are no doubt *Apostles*, for one of those on the east side is certainly St. Peter, as is to be concluded from the fact that he grasps in his left hand a key, the attribute exclusively of the Prince of the Apostles. In front of him is St. Paul; this is confirmed by his high bald forehead and pointed beard, for these are the iconographic characteristics of the Apostle of the Gentiles. It is not possible to name the others with certainty, as none has the particular physiognomy which was to distinguish him in later times, nevertheless one must notice that each personage has characteristics that belong to him alone.

The fact that there are only eight Apostles in the lunettes of the drum is due merely to the law of symmetry which is the dominating factor in the decoration of the chapel, and has prevented the artist from placing three figures in each lunette. It would have been a violation of harmony if, in a lunette with a window in the centre, there had been two figures on the right and only one on the left, or vice versa. This is the reason for which the other four Apostles have been in all probability relegated to the barrel-vaulting of the lateral arms in the midst of trailing acanthus.

In their white robes veined with grey and blue, the figures of the Apostles in the lunettes stand out against a back-ground of intense blue, and therefore give almost the impression of being ghosts and apparitions. Only the change in the lower part of the back-ground to a lighter tint, i.e. a yellowish green, seems to give these figures some sort of footing and a certain sense of spacial depth. Among the Apostles below on the grassy field there are little fountains which doves approach or on the edge of which they stand. These are decorative elements which with time took on an allegorical significance, for it is well known that doves are the symbols of souls and that water alludes to coolness and peace.

The two **lunettes on the east and west sides** have a very

Detail of one of the Apostles

similar composition. Here we see two stags which in order to quench their thirst, proceed through a veritable tangle of acanthus branches towards a pool of water surrounded by a ring of grass and flowers. As we gaze at this simple decoration we spontaneously call to mind the verse of the Psalm which undoubtedly inspired the ancient mosaicist: «As the hart panteth after the fountains of water, so my soul panteth after thee, O Good.» (Psalm XLII vv. 1-2).

The composition of the **lunette above the entrance** is especially impressive. Admist a delightful and varied landscape with rocks, trees, grass and bushes, is a pastoral scene against the back-ground of an early morning sky enlivened with light blue tints. In the centre is the figure of the *Good Shepherd* whom the ancient painters had so often frescoed in the Catacombs. But while in the Catacomb painting the Good Shepherd had almost always been represented as a countryman with short tunic and a stick, here he wears a purple mantle covering a tunic of gold and carrying a tall cross in his left hand. In addition a wide gold halo indicating his divinity shines behind his head; a winning expression of serenity and sweetness illuminates his youthful countenance framed by locks of long hair falling on his shoulders.

On either side of him in similar attitudes stand two groups of sheep facing each other. All are looking towards the mystic Shepherd. He is drawn with long curving lines and forms the real pivot of the scene, not only because he is in the very centre of the lunette, but also because, with head turned to one side and right arm to the other, he attracts to himself the main lines of every part of the composition. But what strikes the visitor most as he moves round this little oratory, is that delicate expanse of colours in the mosaic, which, pervading the entire building, leaves him with a feeling of charmed amazement, for the decoration both as regards range of colour and disposition of the subjects represented, blends perfectly with the architecture.

The artists who decorated the oratory — even if we admit

theoretically, as some have said, that they came from Africa (Duetschke), or from Constantinople (Strzygowski), or from Syria (Diehl), or from Rome (Kurth and Ricci)—undoubtedly took many elements from the art which after Alexander the Great spread in the near East and in the regions conquered by Rome. Therefore they belong uncontestably to the Hellenistico-Roman school (Muratoff) and it is quite possible that the artists were sent for from Milan after the imperial court had left that city for Ravenna.

At the present time the oratory contains **three marble sarcophagi** which were brought here between the 9th century and the beginning of the 14th. The sarcophagus at the further end, beneath the lunette of St. Laurence, is of truly imposing dimensions. Now it has a somewhat bare and rough appearance because the cornice that adorned the margin and those of the middle panel intended for the inscription have been hacked away. The cover consists of two slabs meeting at a point and has triangular finials at the corners. According to tradition it was the sarcophagus which contained the body of Galla Placidia. In fact, the body—as is stated by various authors from the 14th century to the 16th (for example Rinaldo da Concorreggio and G. P. Ferretti)—could be seen through a large aperture (now closed) made in the back of the sarcophagus. If this information is correct the body of Galla Placidia must have been placed seated on a chair of cypress wood. Given this extraordinary attitude, there may be some truth in the theory that a body was put inside the sarcophagus, with the intention of passing it off as that of the Empress, in the 13th or 14th century, a period in which the falsification of relics was common, and tales and legends grew up around them (Gerola, Ricci).

In 1577 some boys, overcome by curiosity, thrust some lighted candles through the opening into the tomb, and the light coming in contact with the planks of cypress wood, destroyed everything, save a few fragments of bone, among them a skull, and a few scraps of wood. This was confirmed by Girolamo Rossi in 1577 and by Corrado Ricci in 1899.

Considering the imposing dimensions of the sarcophagus and the lack of any Christian symbol upon it, it is very probable that it is to be regarded as the pagan coffin of some rich and noble personage.

The sarcophagus which is now in the left arm is called the sarcophagus of Constantius III, Galla Placidia's second husband. It was thus called at the beginning of the 14th century by Rinaldo da Concorreggio, and this was repeated by Desiderio Spreti in the second half of the 15th century. But Girolamo Rossi, towards the end of the 16th century, mentions a belief that the sarcophagus contained the body of Valentinian III, which is supposed to have been brought from Rome to Ravenna. But all these assertions are without foundation, there is no written record and no earlier evidence to confirm them. In 1738 an investigation was made into the contents of the sarcophagus. The cover was removed—says the eye-witness Fiandrini—and disclosed «two entire heads with a few teeth remaining, and bones covered with soft black mud of about three fingers' breadth in depth.»

On the front of the tomb is a very simple scene. In the centre, upon a rock from which four streams gush out, stands a lamb. Its head is surrounded by a halo inscribed with the monogram of Christ—the Greek letters X and P combined. This proves beyond doubt that we have here the mystic Lamb. At the sides of the central figure are two lambs without halos. Probably they stand for Apostles. Two palm trees, one on the right, the other on the left, enclose the composition. This decoration is a motif often used by Christian artists, for the palm—among other things a symbol of victory—recalled verse 13 of Psalm XVI, «Justus ut palma florebit» (The just man shall flourish like a palm tree.)

The scene as a whole is well set on the front of the sarcophagus within an elegant cornice. The lambs are realistically drawn, but the rendering of the fleece shows a conventional handl-

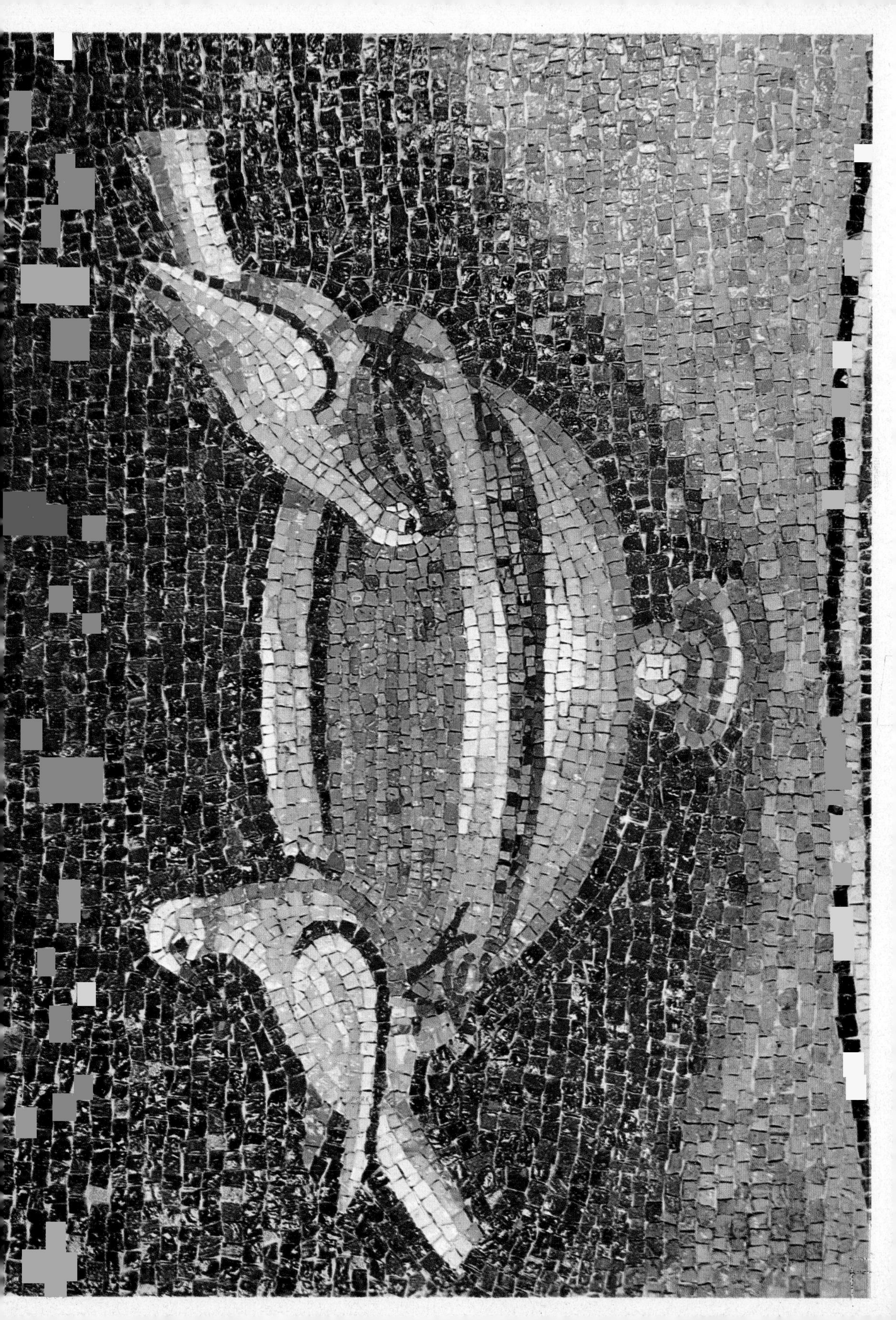

Mausoleo di Galla Placidia: colombe (V sec.)

Mausoleo di Galla Placidia: Doves (5th cent.)

ing. Stylised elements are also to be noticed in the treatment of the two palms. This sarcophagus may be attributed to about the end of the 5th century. The sarcophagus in the right arm of the oratory is held by some (Rinaldo da Concorreggio), to be of Valentinian III, son of Galla Placidia and Constantius III, and by others (G. Rossi) as that of the Emperor Honorius. But these attributions are also without foundation. In 1738 the bones of two persons, some those of a woman, were to be seen in this sarcophagus.

The front of this coffin, the corners of which are adorned by small fluted columns, has three niches. The lateral ones are exactly alike, and have two spirally fluted columns surmounted by an arch enclosing a shell; below is carved a cross. The shrine in the centre has no arch but a pointed roof; here one sees a tall cross on the lateral arms of which perch two doves. It rests on the rock from which flow the four symbolical rivers, and on it stands the divine Lamb seen in profile with head turned back over the body. The back of the sarcophagus bears a design like that on the front save for some small details, but it is merely sketched.

The cover is of semicylindrical form and the carving represents overlapping scales. It is entirely surrounded by a cornice showing a plait enclosing ovoids. This sarcophagus is to be attributed to the beginning of the 6th century.

S. Vitale

S. VITALE

The Church of S. Vitale has always awakened the liveliest admiration. Indeed, while in the first half of the 9th century Andrea-Agnello wrote that no building in Italy could be compared with S. Vitale as regards the form and plan of the edifice, Choisy, the well known historian, could declare, during the last century, that never had stability, originality, splendour of colour and purity of line—the genius of Rome and that of the East—been associated in such a fascinating and harmonious whole.

The Church was begun by Bishop Ecclesius after his return from his mission to Byzantium in 525 together with Pope John. For this reason it is considered that the building was commenced in the reign of Amalasuntha, who succeeded her father Theodoric in 526, and adopted a policy of wider toleration towards the Catholics.

Reliable historical information tells us that the funds required for building (it cost 26000 «soldi» of gold) were put at the disposal of the Bishop by Julianus Argentarius; we do not know exactly who this influential personage was. It has been said that he was the architect of the building (Rivoira, Lugli) and also the treasurer of the Church in Ravenna (Von Quast, Ricci), but these theories have now been rejected, and it seems more likely that he was a wealthy private banker (Hartmann, Rosenberg, Schubart and Deichmann), though we need not entirely exclude the idea that may have been at the same time a sort of «longa manus» of Justinian (Testi-Rasponi, Von Simson), that is, one charged by the Emperor to act in Ravenna as a kind of fifth column, with the duty of preparing the ground, thus facilitating the conquest of the city by the Byzantines, who occupied it in the year 540.

The Church, though begun by the Goths, was finished under the Byzantines, for it was consecrated in May 547, if not, as is perhaps more likely, in 548 (Testi-Rasponi), but its founder, Bishop Ecclesius, did not live to see the completion of the building, nor did his immediate successors, the Bishops Ursicinus and Victor, since we know that the solemn consecration of the church took place during the episcopate of Maximian, the great ruler born at Pola who was the first in Ravenna to assume the title of Archbishop.

The edifice, which has an octagonal plan, is built with the typical bricks somewhat long and thin, which were used only in the buildings erected by Julianus Argentarius. The exterior reveals the way in which the space within is divided, for the upper and narrower part, covered with a pyramidal roof, hides and protects the cupola, while the lower and wider part allows for two ambulatories or arcades around the walls, one upon the ground floor and the other, the *matroneum*, above it.

The rhythmic regularity of line imparted by the octagonal plan is even more conspicuous in the apse as a whole, for it is flanked by the *prothesis* and *diaconicon* (the two small chapels typical of Byzantine sacred edifices) which, with their varied play of volume, throw into relief the emphasis on height shown by the architectural forms on this side.

Almost opposite the apse is the *narthex*, or ancient entrance to the church. The form is that of a porch with semicircular side walls, facing each other in a way suggesting a pair of pincers. In front of it there was originally an atrium, of which Maioli found

S. Vitale

some traces during the last century. This narthex is not in line with the main axis of the church, for it does not stand against the side of octagon which faces the apse, but is on one of the angles. It is therefore linked with the two sides which meet at that point by the two triangular spaces which result, and at the wide end of these rise the two round towers in which were the stairways leading to the matroneum in ancient times.

This curious position of the porch with regard to the building has been explained in various ways. Some scholars have thought that it was due to the presence on the site of some small chapels for which—despite their destruction because of their being within the area of the new building—a respectful memory was necessary (Ricci, Gerola). Others have held that the expedient was determined by the desire to give the entrance a more imposing appearance, and at the same time to find a solution of the problem which would enable the towers to be more closely united with the main building (Jackson). Moreover there have not been wanting some who think that this unsymmetrical arrangement was due solely to artistic or structural reasons (Jonescu). Others—perhaps with closer adherence to reality—have found the explanation in the opportunity gained of making two doorways on two sides of the octagon, instead of the single opening afforded by one side (Toesca).

The **interior** of the church is the more impressive because, though the shadow is deepest and lingers more in the two colonnades along the walls, the central space is flooded with light. This contrast gives rise to a strange pictorial effect which is greatly increased by the alternation of space and mass afforded by the eight tall massive pillars that support the cupola, and alternate with the wide window spaces that seem intended to make the architectural structure as little material as possible.

Particular mention must be made of the great cupola, not, certainly, for the late 18th century frescoes, which, not to mention other defects, give a wrong impression of the structure—but

S. Vitale (sec. VI) - il Cristo dell'arco trionfale
S. Vitale: Christ (Detail from the triumphal arch)

S. Vitale - The vaulting of the choir

rather for the system with which it was carried out. The architect, in fact, not only achieved his object by making use of the usual light material consisting of terracotta tubes inserted one within the other and placed horizontally in double rows to form circles growing smaller and smaller as one row was placed upon another, but also by striving to diminish the lateral pressure as much as possible. To this end he considered it best to make the weight of the great cover fall as far as possible on the eight massive pillars below, by giving the cupola a conical outline that tended to get the pressure of the whole exercised rather in a vertical direction.

According to some scholars the architecture of S. Vitale is the last expression in the West of the constructive methods and spacial forms typical of Roman art (Rivoira, Bettini); others, on the contrary, think that it represents one of the most characteristic examples of Byzantine architectural genius (Strzygowski, Diehl).

In our modest opinion a compromise is possible between these two contrasting theories, not because this is one of the simplest ways of solving the problem, but because it answers effectively to concrete and positive facts. We must remember that Bishop Ecclesius began building the church on his return from the East where he must have been impressed by more than one of the churches with central plan, and such churches were rather rare in the West. By this we do not intend to deny that oriental building with concentric plan derived in their turn from western systems of building, but in them some features genuinely their own were undoubtedly elaborated. It is therefore our personal opinion that, both as regards plan as well as structure, S. Vitale is, after all, a Roman building; but the fount of inspiration is not to be found in Italy, but rather in eastern regions.

Moreover, one should remember the circumstance that in S. Vitale certain architectural features typically Byzantine are to be found, such as the « pulvini » and capitals, the latter of which show open-work, in that the surface carving has been cut away and isolated from the stone behind, thus produc-

MAXIMIANVS

Basilica di S. Vitale - L'Imperatore Giustiniano con il seguito
Basilica of St. Vitale: Emperor Justinian with ritenue

Right side of the sanctuary

ing the appearance of a light embroidery rich in geometrical motifs and plant designs.

The **mosaic decoration** is all concentrated in the deep well-lit choir and apse. We have here an artistic complex of the highest order, due to the activity of two different artistic schools. The work in the choir is that of a school trained in the Hellenistico-Roman tradition; the mosaicists of the apse were of pure Byzantine education. We can be sure of this by noting the principal differences; in the mosaics of the choir the personages are figured in the most varied positions, some are seen in frontal attitude, some in profile, some half way between the two; some are standing, others are seated, some are bending down, others standing erect, some are resting, others are in movement. In the mosaics of the apse, on the other hand, all the personages—excepting only the Christ in the centre of the cupola—are always shown in frontal position, always standing upright, always stiff and motionless.

Beneath the clothing of the figures in the choir we can often catch a glimpse of the anatomical structure of the body, we often note the form of the limbs. Nothing of this can be seen in the figures in the mosaics in the apse; on the contrary, the garments seem to fall rigidly like cloaks of metal. Again, in the choir the personages stand out against a lively landscape with rocks, trees and clouds. In other words the scene is drawn direct from nature. But behind the figures of the apse we see only an unbroken expanse of gold which offers no sylvan landscape, but rather seems to lift the scene to a trascendental plane which might be said to lie beyond time and space.

But these undeniable differences do not imply that it is necessary to assign the two groups of mosaics to different epochs. One might rather say that they were executed about the same time, those of the choir being perhaps a little earlier than those of the apse.

The truth is that in the same period artists were living who followed quite different ideals. There was—as there is today—a

S. Vitale - The mosaic decoration in the dome of the apse

crossing and interweaving of various currents. As a result, we may say that in S. Vitale the decoration of the apse was entrusted to workers who found their pictorial ideal in an artistic world quite different from that which inspired the mosaicists who planned the ornamentation of the walls and vaulting of the choir.

The *Choir*. Access is marked by a great arch on the intrados of which on a dark background there are fifteen medaillons which start from the summit where the figure of the *Redeemer* is seen, and contain gold haloed busts of the *Twelve Apostles* and two others, presumed to be the sons of St. Vitalis, the *Saints Gervasius* and *Protasius*. Each medaillon is separated from the next by two dolphins with tails crossed, and is surrounded by a series of lively luminous motifs showing globes and crosses.

The decoration on the left wall is, like that on the right, marked by great naturalism; moreover, there is a strict correspondence between the two walls as regards the plan of the composition.

On the left side, above the great «trifora» (or two-pillared opening into the lower ambulatory) the space is filled by a large lunette in which we see *two episodes in the life of Abraham*; first, the Patriarch is seen offering hospitality to the three Angels who announce to him and his wife Sarah, seen standing on the threshold of the hut, the birth of a son, and then the sacrifice of that son, Isaac, by Abraham who hastens thus to obey God's will. Not only are the two scenes wonderfully adapted to the curve of the lunette, they are also noteworthy for certain details in the treatment of the figures. Above all it is interesting to observe the masterly manner and fine taste with which the artist has avoided the usual uniformity in the position of the three seated Angels by slightly inclining the heads of the lateral ones, and above all in the varied positions of their hands and feet. Beautiful too is the group showing Abraham about to complete the sacrifice, because of its pyramidal scheme which has at the summit the drawn sword of the Patriarch, and at the extremities of the base, the altar upon

Detail of the mosaic of the apse

which is the half-kneeling figure of little Isaac, and the ram which after the testing of Abraham, is to take the place of the human victim.

Above the arch of the lunette are *two Angels in flight* who hold a disc enclosing a cross. On the left side we see the *Prophet Jeremiah,* a large scroll in his hands, while on the right, low down, are the representatives of the *twelve tribes of Israel* grouped round Aaron, and higher up, *Moses* in the act of ascending the rocky slopes of Mt. Sinai to receive the Law from the hand of God which reaches out from a long bank of clouds.

In the upper zone, beside the fine «trifora» with its two magnificent alabaster columns surmounted by beautifully carved capitals, we see two of the Evangelists—*St. John and St. Luke*— who are depicted in the midst of a naturalistic scene not wanting in stylised elements, awaiting inspiration to write their Gospels; this is the reason why a short of small table with pens and ink-stand is seen beside them. They are grave and solemn personages who wear purple-bordered tunics and white mantles, while at their feet ducks and other aquatic birds swim on limpid waters. Above the heads of the two Evangelists appear their respective symbols: the Eagle and the Bull.

Above the arch of the «trifora» on the outer side there is a decoration of vine branches which spring from two large vases and unfold in a series of volutes or coils. A similar decoration is seen above the arches of the upper «trifora» on the opposite wall, and a composition—exactly corresponding to the one mentioned above—is seen in the lateral zones in which appear the Evangelists—*St. Matthew and St. Mark*—shown in about the same position as the other two. Above them are their symbols: the Angel and the Lion, and below them again are aquatic creatures, among the most charming of which are a heron and a tortoise.

The great lunette above the *lower* «trifora» is surmounted by the usual design of *two Angels in flight*. On their right is the *Prophet Isaia,* and on the left, down below, we see *Moses watch-*

S. Vitale - The mosaic decoration on the South wall of the choir

ing the flocks of his father-in-law, and above *Moses unfastening his sandals to approach the burning Bush*, which is shown by bright tongues of flame arising from a rocky ground.

Within the lunette—as in the one in front—two scenes are shown; they are the *Sacrifice of Abel and that of Melchizedek*. The two men advance, the one from the left the other from the right, towards an altar raised on four small columns and completely covered with an embroidered cloth. Abel, who stands near a poor hut and a tree edged along the trunk and the leafy top with a gleam of white, is clad in a short skin and a bright red cloak; he carries a lamb on his arm. Melchizedek, behind whom stands a sumptuos temple, wears rich garments reaching to his feet; he advances with a loaf of bread, and is looking upwards to the point where the hand of God appears among the clouds.

It has justly been observed that the composition in this lunette, though airy and not without organic structure, is perhaps to be considered somewhat inferior to the opposite one showing scenes in the life of Abraham (Toesca). But in any case the subjects in both are well suited to the place they occupy, for, being at the sides of the altar, they seem artistically to join in the beautiful prayer which, both in ancient days and in our own, is repeated by the priest at Mass after the Consecration: «Above them (the bread and the wine) do Thou vouchsafe to look with favourable and gracious countenance and accept them, as Thou didst vouchsafe to accept the gifts of Thy just servant Abel, and the sacrifice of our Patriarch Abraham, and that which Thy High Priest Melchizedek offered unto Thee, a holy Sacrifice, an unspotted Victim».

The choir has a ribbed cross-vaulting bearing a luxurious decoration which covers it so completely that one might say the artist must have had a real horror of empty spaces—*horror vacui*. Along the ascending lines of the triangles rise four bands adorned with leaves and fruit meeting at the summit in a wreath which encloses the white figure of the *Lamb of God* (*Agnus Dei*) stand-

Basilica di S. Vitale - L'Imperatrice Teodora con la sua Corte
Basilica of St. Vitale: Empress Theodora with her Court

ing out against a sky lit up by a myriad stars. Towards this central medallion also converge the lifted arms of four Angels who stand upon azure globes and set in the midst of a green expanse of acanthus branches, whose coils are brightened with gold and give the impression of being as it were lightly touched by continual vibrations of air and light.

Here in the choir the whole decoration is inspired by nature, and the colour lends its powerful aid to impart vigour and freshness to the various figures.

More tense is the colour of the mosaics of the choir arch where there is an unbroken background of gold against which we see the two *Angels,* flying in a horizontal position and holding up a disc crossed by eight rays of light which come from a central Alpha. At the sides of these angels are two green cypress trees, and then a representation of the *City of Jerusalem and the City of Bethlehem* with walls studded with gems and precious stones; they are symbols respectively of the Church of the Jews and the Church of the Gentiles.

It is a truly divine vision that we see in the dome of the apse. On a field dotted with flowers and varied by two layers of rocks lying one upon the other, while four symbolical rivers gush forth from the centre, stand five personages. In the centre is the *Redeemer*, young and beardless, seated upon a globe of vivid blue. Beside him stand *two Archangels.* He is clad entirely in purple and his halo is signed with a cross. In his left hand he holds the scroll with the seven seals, and with his right he offers the triumphal crown to *St. Vitalis* who advances from the left ready to receive it with hands covered with his mantle. From the opposite side comes *Bishop Ecclesius*, carrying a model of the church he had begun, the form of which is that which the church actually has.

All these figures are of the same height and are set against a gold back-ground which is enlivened above by the presence of thin whitish blue and whitish pink clouds, and these, relieving the radiant splendour of the wide surface with its metallic glow, by introducing a naturalistic touch, may be due to the suggestion of a local artist.

As the vault of the apse displays the court of Heaven, so, lower down in the two sections at the side, we see the earthly court with all the pomp and ostentation of the East.

In the left one is seen the *Emperor Justinian* who carries a gold paten in his hands. Preceded by a subdeacon swinging a censer, a deacon carrying the Book of the Gospels, and Bishop Maximian—the only person to have his name written above his head—the Emperor is seen accompanied by three high dignitaries and is followed by soldiers of the guard.

All these persons are shown full-face, stiff and static, their figures, without solidity of form, seem to have become incorporeal, fixed in simple rhythmic expressions. One has almost the feeling that the slow procession has made a right about face, but only in order to let itself be admired for a few minutes, the pause will be brief, the slow advance may be resumed at any moment.

The colour in the garments of these personages is widely spread, especially as regards the white and the purple. Yet a heightening of tone by means of brilliant colours is not wanting; it is provided by the bright tints—greens and reds—of the soldiers' garment. In this panel the figures which most attract attention are those of Justinian and Maximian; the former, with diadem and nimbus, represents the temporal power («regalis potestas»), the second, with pallium and cross, the attributes of episcopal rank, stands for the spiritual power («sacrata auctoritas»).

The countenance of Justinian must certainly have been drawn according to the fixed conventions for imperial portraits that were sent out into the provinces, but that of Maximian was certainly delineated by an artist who knew the real features of the Bishop; so this emaciated face, with its clearly marked

Basilica di S. Vitale - Particolare decorativo del Presbiterio
Basilica of St. Vitale: Mosaics of the choir (detail)

Sarcophagus of Isaacius

characteristics and enlivened by penetrating blue eyes may be taken to be the finest portrait among all those preserved in the mosaics of Ravenna. Looking again at the Bishop's slender figure, the head with its scanty locks of hair, and the face lit up by the blue eyes—which caused a famous Italian painter (Severini) to compare it with one of Cezanne's self-portraits—one recalls the words with which the first historian, Andrea-Agnello, described the saintly Bishop: «He was of tall stature, thin in face, bald-headed save for a few locks of hair, with grey-blue eyes, and adorned with every grace».

Among the other persons who appear in the panel, and who may be said simply to form the imperial retinue, there is one who seems to have a certain importance; he is the one, with features so typically original as certainly to be taken from life, who is seen between the Emperor and the Bishop in the second plane. We do not know precisely who he was; some critics have suggested that he is Julianus Argentarius (Testi-Rasponi, Von Simson, Rodenwaldt), but recently this supposition has been doubted as improbable, and the latest theory—taking into consideration also the particular position this personage occupies in the picture—is that here we see the «Praetorius» of Italy, the high functionary who represented the imperial authority at the consecration of the church (Deichmann).

The picture on the right, facing the one with the figure of Justinian, represents the *Empress Theodora*, who advances with a golden chalice studded with gems in her hands. She is preceded by two civil dignitaries and is followed by a crowd of court ladies. She seems rather about to leave the throne room of her palace than to be on the point of entering the church (Visser, Cecchelli).

In this panel, as in the other, the wide expanses of white and purple are again used, but here too the colour becomes vivid and brilliant, as can be seen in the glowing silk robes of the ladies,

Basilica di S. Vitale - Particolare decorativo del Presbiterio

Basilica of St. Vitale: Mosaics of the choir (detail)

which, by the brightness of their colours seem to catch the leitmotiv of that blue, white and red curtain hanging above.

Theodora, adorned with a rich diadem set with pearls and gems, is wrapped in an ample purple mantle the lower part of which is embroidered in gold with the scene of the Wise Men bringing their gifts to the Holy Child. There is no doubt that the artist, by introducing this scene into the Empress's robe, wished to suggest an obvious comparison, wished in fact to express this idea: «As the Wise Men bring gifts to the Child Jesus, so we, Justinian and Theodora, offer our gifts to Christ» (Grabar). Thus it is clear that the scenes in the two panels are not so much—as Tea has said—a representation of the offering which in ancient times the faithful used to make after the reading of the Gospel, as a representation of the «oblatio Augusti et Augustae» i.e. that gift of liturgical vessels which the Byzantine Emperors often made to the most important churches in the territories over which they ruled.

While in the panel showing Justinian there are two conspicuous persons, as we have seen, in the panel showing Theodora there is only one who dominates the scene; it is the Empress herself, who is taller than the other ladies.

Since it has been noticed that only the first two ladies who follow Theodora have expressive faces, while the others all have the same stereotyped look, an attempt has been made to name these two ladies. A not improbable theory identifies them as Antonina and Giovannina, wife and daughter of Belisarius who had conquered Ravenna; this is all the more likely as we learn from the historian Procopius of Caesarea, that they were the Empress's intimate friends.

It is to be noted how all the figures, by now devoid of any material reality, have no value here save that of rhythm of line and the repeated cadences of a musical composition, and how the colour reaches its highest brilliance in the display of enamel and mother-of-pearl which, by the small size of the «tesserae» and their varied arrangement, give rise to a striking interplay of a thousand lights and a thousand reflexions.

On the side walls of the choir, very close to the great arch that gives access to it, are inserted two marble fragments that formed part of the so-called «Throne of Neptune», a sculpture of the Hellenistico-Roman age. They show cherubs bearing the attributes of some divinities against an architectural background.

In the circular chapel to the right of the apse a few interesting objects have been preserved: a small *casket* of the 6th century bearing the name of Julianus Argentarius; the broken *sarcophagus of Bishop Ecclesius*, its front adorned with a flat relief showing a cross flanked by two stags, two peacocks and two palms; and a *sarcophagus* of the second half of the 5th century, which, shortly before the middle of the 7th, was used again, to receive the remains (so says the Greek inscription carved on the rounded lid) of the *Exarch Isaccius*. Upon the smooth background of the front of this sarcophagus a few figures in somewhat high relief are roughly carved: they are Wise Men in typical oriental costume—breeches and short tunics with Phrygian caps on their heads—bringing their gifts to the Child Jesus who is seated on the Madonna's knees.

THE NATIONAL MUSEUM

Close by the church of S. Vitale stands the National Museum which is reached from the grassy expanse that lies before the entrance into the church. One enters through a small but elegant portico with Verona red columns. On the lintel of the graceful 16th century doorway are carved the words of Virgil: «Procul o procul este prophani». The Museum occupies the cloister of the ex-Benedictine monastery, and is due to the amalgamation, carried out by the sculptor Enrico Pazzi, of the collections made by the monks of Classe and those of S. Vitale, with certain modern collections.

In the **first cloister** which in the sober lines of its architecture bears the stamp of fine Renaissance art, the objects are mainly of a funerary character, and were placed here in 1950: some *sarcophagus fronts*, some *sepulchral pillars* (*stele*) with portraits of the dead persons and various funeral tablets. Many of these, carved on rectangular slabs, belong to the «classiarii» i.e. the soldiers of the Roman fleet stationed in the Port of Classe. Almost all of them were discovered in the 18th century, not far from S. Apollinare in Classe, where, before the church was built, there was a large cemetery. The inscriptions on them are very simple but exceedingly interesting. As a rule they give not only the names of the soldiers and the places whence they came

(Egypt, Syria, Dalmatia etc.), but also a record of the ships in which they served, their age and the length of service.

The series of funeral pillars is especially worthy of note. Some of them bear portraits of the dead men, and of the members of their households, including freedmen and slaves. The most famous among them is the one in three storeys made at the beginning of the 1st century A.D. for himself and his family by a certain Publius Longidienus, who was, as the inscription tells us, a ship's carpenter («faber navalis»). Moreover he wished to be shown on the lower part of the monument in the act of working with an axe on a ship which is being built and which is seen standing upon three high supports.

Very interesting also—especially for the vigour of some of its portraits—is the «stele» in four storeys belonging to the families Firmia and Latronia.

Near the «stele» of Publius Longidienus is the famous sculpture in marble: the *relief with the portraits of members of the Julius-Claudian Family.* Some of the personages still keep the secret of their identity, yet according to the latest studies (M. Santangelo), the individuals, reading from right to left, seem to be as follows: Augustus, Livia, Marcellus, Agrippa, and a seated female deity. It is a fine and accurate piece of work, and translates into relief the contemporary products of the statuary art (Strong).

In a room whose entrance is beside this relief all the existing marble remains of the *Porta Aurea* have been placed. This gate in the walls of Ravenna was built in 43 A.D. by the Emperor Claudius. Among the fragments the ones most worthy of mention are the two great circular «patere», or discs, adorned with an exterior ring of bead and reel ornament, a wreath of oak leaves and a wide band with palm motifs.

Along the walls of the **second cloister** with its fine columns grouped in pairs—the work of Andrea da Valle, a disciple of Falconetto—we see arranged in chronological order, sculpture fragments of early Christian, Byzantine, Romanesque, Gothic, Renaissance and Baroque art. Among the most interesting pieces may

The National Museum: Ceramic plate of the factory of Castelli with a scene of a triumph

be mentioned the *Sarcophagus of the Traditio Legis* which belongs to the early years of the 5th century (the sculpture shows Christ granting the primacy of his church to St. Peter, to whom he hands the book of the Law); there are also some *capitals* from the demolished church of S. Andrea dei Goti; in one of these, amid large acanthus leaves which seem to be blown out by the wind, is the monogram of the words «Theodericus Rex».

The **small rooms** which follow one another **on the first floor** of this second cloister contain materials of very different kinds. Note-worthy are some *Greek portraits* (among them Miltiades, Epicurus and Carneades) which were found on various occasions, from 1936, in the Adriatic about five miles out at sea between Porto Corsini and the mouth of the river Reno. They seem to have formed part of a cargo of works of art coming from Rome whence they were sent in the second half of the 16th century by the younger Cardinal Ippolito d'Este to the Duke Alfonso d'Este at Ferrara. They were cast into the sea when the ship in which they were being carried was in danger of sinking, or else they went down with the ship. They were all Roman copies of those ornamental heads which were often used to adorn the villas and libraries of the ancients.

In the **so-called Byzantine room** we note especially four fine «*transenne*» or large open-work panels of the 6th century, three of which certainly came from S. Vitale. The marble is cut rather than sculptured, thus producing a lively colouristic effect resembling black and white. Thanks to the great skill of those who executed the trepanning, the marble surface comes to resemble embroidery with fantastic designs of stylised leaves, branches and coils which take on a rigid appearance as if they had undergone a process of cristallization. The symbolic motifs grafted on to these intricate patterns—such as peacocks, crosses and doves—seem almost to lay aside their religious significance, in order the better to attain an exquisitely pictorial and supremely decorative effect.

Another celebrated work of sculpture in this room—which also contains the original *bronze cross* that surmounted the roof

Five sided cover of Murano (Ivory)

of S. Vitale till 1911—is the great bas-relief representing the third of the twelve labours of Hercules: *the capture of the Deer* (here it is clearly a stag). The relief, which goes back perhaps to the end of the 5th century, is of particular importance, because, if the scheme is inspired by the models of Greek art of the 4th century B.C., the rendering reveals the essential spirit of Byzantine art: to transform plasticity into pictorial sculpture.

The same intention is seen in the fine open-work *capital*—a work not much earlier than the middle of the 6th century—which came from the destroyed church of S. Michele in Africisco.

Very important too are the *circular window-panels* of various brilliant colours. They are from the windows of the apse of S. Vitale, and must be considered the most ancient specimens of window-glass belonging to a church (Cecchelli).

The **collection of stuffs** from Coptic to Renaissance specimens, boasts two pieces that are very famous, both being assigned to the 9th century. The first is the so-called «Velo di Classe»; it consists of three lengths embroidered with various busts of Veronese Bishops. Originally intended for the altar of the relics of the Saints Fermo and Rustico at Verona, it was eventually brought to the Ravennate monastery at Classe. The second piece comes from the tomb of S. Giuliano at Rimini: it is fine silk material, now brown in colour, with two rows of small circles; in the centre of each of these a lion seems lightly and watchfully to advance; the form of these animals and of the other decorative motifs which adorn the stuff recalls the art of the Sassanid dynasty of Persian Kings.

The **collection of ivories** is one of the most precious sections of the Museum, there are specimens of remote and of recent times. The most ancient, perhaps of the 5th century or the early 6th, is the one showing *Apollo with his cithern and Daphne*. It is not impossible, considering the subject, that it was the cover of one of those containers mentioned by the grammarian Papia, intended for love letters. It may be of Egyptian origin (Volbach). The same origin is attributed to the *cover for the Evangelistary* which was brought from the Camaldolese monastery of S. Mi-

The so-called Apotheosis of Augustus

Roman sarcophagus

P·LONGIDIENVS·P·L·RVFIO
P·LONGIDIENVS·P·L·PILADES
INPENSA·A·PATRONO·DEDERVNT
P·LONGIDIENVS
P·F·AD·ONVS
PROPERAT

The National Museum - The Roman funeral stele of Publius Longidienus ◀

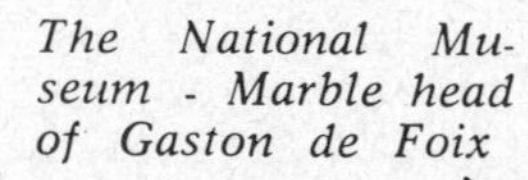

The National Museum - Marble head of Gaston de Foix ▶

The National Museum:
A piece of stuff discovered in the sarcophagus of S. Giuliano in Rimini ▼

chele at Murano to the one at Classe. It consists of five parts, and is sometimes referred to as «the five-sided cover of Murano». It bears a representation of Christ enthroned above the scene of the three young Hebrews in the furnace. Around we see four of the miracles of Jesus, and underneath, two episodes from the story of Jonah.

The **collection of ceramics** also comprises precious treasures, for there are products of the most celebrated factories, from those of Deruta to those of Faenza, from those of Urbino to those of Castelli. The most noted of all are two large plates in metallic lustre ware; they are of Hispano-Moorish workmanship belonging to the last quarter of the 15th century, and are decorated with a series of small leaves arranged in concentric circles. One has a ram in the centre, and the other the sign of Capricorn.

There is a very original cup from Faenza belonging to the 15th century; it was found in 1914 in the excavation of St. Agatha. Its enamel is of exquisite workmanship and it retains an uncommon transparency of colour. It is a loving cup bearing the figure of a woman holding a book in her right hand, and in her left a cup containing two eyes. Near the outer edge runs the Latin inscription beginning: «Faciat unusquisque quod vult sive...» (Let each do as he will or...». Around the bottom we read an inscription which consists of a combination of letters and musical notes in the usual four clefs in key F. It is a love song which ends with the lament: «Tu solla sei che mi fai languire cum la mia faretra che mi passato il core sol fa mio possente amore già non posso abandonare» (Thou alone art she who makes me languish with my quiver, who hast pierced my heart so that I cannot now abandon my great love).

The Museum possesses also a rich **collection of Creto-Venetian icons** of the period from the 14th century to the 18th, and a valuable **numismatic section** containing more than 6600 specimens. Among them are some gold coins of Galla Placidia and Justinian, and also some medals by Pisanello and Benvenuto Cellini.

THE CATHEDRAL

Of the ancient Cathedral of Ravenna, originally dedicated to the «Aghia Anastasis» i.e. the Resurrection of the Lord, hardly anything remains. The present building (196 ft. long) has a central nave and two aisles and goes back little further than the middle of the 18th century. It was built by the Riminese architect Gian Francesco Buonamici, after he had first, by order of Archbishop Farsetti, demolished the ancient Ursian Basilica with its five naves supported by 56 columns; this building had, however, been considerably altered from time to time during the course of the centuries.

The ancient church—the largest within the walls of Ravenna's civic limits, was built, as the name implies, by Bishop Ursus who must have occupied the episcopal throne, not in the last years of the 4th century, as some scholars think (Bjvanck, Bettini), but during the first decades of the 5th (Testi-Rasponi). It is indeed natural to connect the building of that magnificent edifice with the changed conditions in Ravenna, after the Emperor Honorius had transferred his court thither from Milan, at the beginning of the 5th century, since, at that time, it must have been considered incompatible with the Emperor's residence that the Christian community should continue to meet—as says the first historian Andrea-Agnello—«in huts» i.e. in small oratories or at least in very modest buildings.

The investigations carried out in 1731 made it possible to establish the fact that the earliest level of the church's mosaic pavement (a fragment of which is preserved in the Archiepiscopal Museum) is to be found about 10 ft. below the present one. Moreover at the beginning of this century Gerola was able to ascertain that the apse of the early building (in part preserved beneath the existing apse, but no longer visible) backed on to a part of the wall of the Roman city. The vault of the apse was originally adorned with mosaics, but these must have been destroyed a few centuries later, because in 1112 the entire decoration of the apse was renewed. These new mosaics were destroyed in 1734 by Buonamici, after he himself had made a drawing in order to preserve a record of them. Now only a few fragments remain and these are to be seen in the Archiepiscopal Museum.

Not just before the opening of the 12th century (Ricci), but rather near the end of the 10th (Gerola, Verzone) a spacious crypt was built beneath the choir; it can no longer be visited as it is always full of water. It is of the type which stands between those of semianular form and those that have the form of an oratory. The central part is roofed by cross vaulting having ribs, while it finishes at the end in barrel-vaulting, partly resting on marble columns of varying sizes, surmounted by capitals or «pulvini» each different from the others. It is clear that this material came from other buildings.

The erection of the **Campanile** is assigned to about the same period as the crypt; it is a round bell-tower and is about 115 ft. high. Its original level was more than 6 ft. below the present. As the historian Andrea-Agnello—so scrupulous in giving details relating to the churches of Ravenna—never mentions bell-towers, it has been thought that they were not built till after his time, and that they belong to a period between the 9th century and the 11th. In any case, the oldest historical information at present known concerning the bell-towers of Ravenna is that which refers to the work done in 1038 to the bell-tower of the Cathedral by Archbishop Gebeardo.

With regard to the round form of several of Ravenna's bell-

The mosaic decoration of the 13th century which adorned the apse and the arch of the choir in the ancient Ursian Basilica (from a drawing of the architect Buonamici of the 18th century)

towers, it is held to be derived from that of the towers containing stairways, seen in the city walls e.g. the cylindrical towers, so well known, which flanked the Porta Aurea till the end of the 15th century.

In the **interior** of the Cathedral several works of early Christian and Byzantine sculpture are preserved.

A sarcophagus of about the middle of the 5th century is used as a front for the third altar of the right aisle. Now it contains the bones of the Bishops Esuperantius and Maximian. On its face it shows *Christ between two Apostles*; beyond them are also two palm trees laden with dates.

Of the second half of the 5th century are the two imposing sarcophagi seen in the **Chapel of the Blessed Virgin (Vergine del Sudore)** at the end of the right transept. More ancient is the one in which the body of *Archbishop Rinaldo da Concorreggio* was laid in 1321. The scene carved on the front is so impressive that—as Toesca justly says—it would seem to have derived from some vast mural decoration rather than to have been conceived for the narrow front of a sarcophagus. Here Christ is seen enthroned and motionless upon the mount from which flow the four symbolical rivers. In his left hand he holds the open book, while with his right he welcomes St. Peter and St. Paul who hasten to him with rapid steps, bearing on their hands covered with their cloaks the signs of martyrdom and victory. This subject, which is well spaced out, is framed at the sides by two stiff palm trees identical even in their crescent-shaped mass of foliage, and above by light clouds. These naturalistic features do not give an effect of landscape, but, with their calculated symmetry and planned rhythmical quality they seem to have their part in this solemn vision. The sarcophagus has a heavy arched lid, of the type also called «a baule» (like a trunk).

The *sarcophagus of St. Barbatianus* is now so called because the bones of Galla Placidia's confessor and advisor were placed within it in 1658. The front is partitioned into niches, and here, for the last time in the early Christian sculpture preserved at Ravenna, we see Christ between S. Peter and St. Paul. The three

The Cathedral - The pulpit erected by Bishop Agnellus (6th century)

Sarcophagus

figures are perfectly frontal, and they are completely independent of one another. Their eyes are fixed on vacancy, the drapery of their garments is formalised, their attitudes rigid. One might almost say that both Christ and the Apostles have assumed the appearance of ghosts. In each of the two lateral niches is a vase with curved handles from which springs a plant resembling a lily just coming into leaf.

Very famous and important for the history of Byzantine sculpture is the marble **pulpit** about half way along the central nave on the right hand. On the two sides runs an inscription which reads: «Servus Xpi Agnellus episc. hunc pyrgum fecit» (The servant of Christ Bishop Agnellus made this pulpit). From it we learn that the sculpture goes back to the time of Archbishop Agnellus (556-569). We have here a characteristic type of pulpit in Greek marble resembling a low tower which is elliptical instead of cylindrical; it is divided into two almost equal parts by means of two openings in which, between sloping parapets, steps were laid. The decoration is the same on both sides: horizontal and vertical friezes crossing at right angles divide the surface into 36 panels set in six horizontal zones. In each panel is carved an animal which varies from zone to zone; working from the top downwards, we see: a lamb, a peacock, a stag, a dove, a duck, and a fish. The idea which inspired it is typically Byzantine, because based on the constant monotonous repetition of the same decorative motifs, which, though they have a symbolic meaning, seem to fade into a merely ornamental repetition. The animals, flat and devoid of plasticity, stand out on a small smooth field within their panel.

Among the works of art of more recent times we may mention the **Chapel of the Blessed Sacrament** at the further end of the left transept. Built in the early 17th century according to the design of Carlo Maderno, it was frescoed by Guido Reni and some of his disciples.

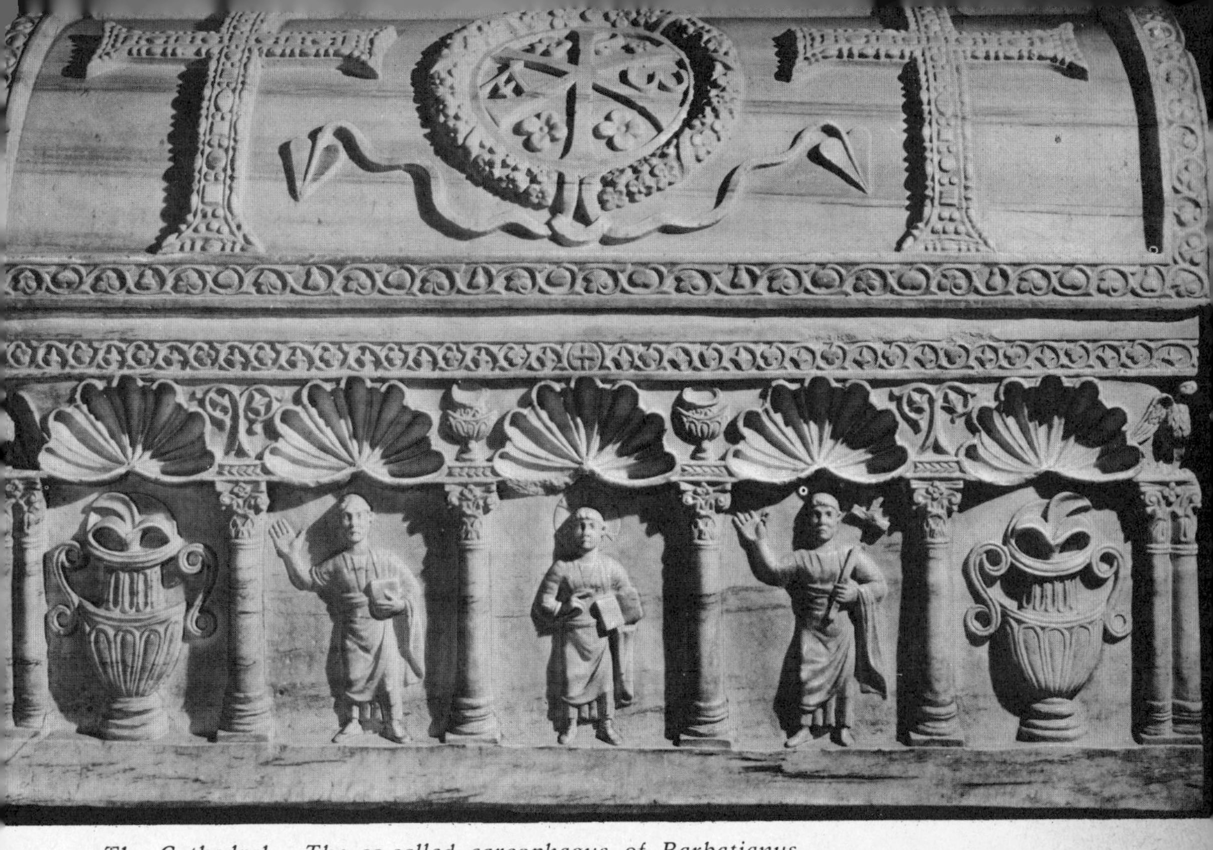

The Cathedral - The so-called sarcophagus of Barbatianus

Sarcophagus of Archbishop Rinaldo da Concorreggio

The Cathedral Baptistery

Battistero della Cattedrale: Interno
Cathedral Baptistery: Interior

THE CATHEDRAL BAPTISTERY

This Baptistery, which has a diameter of about 36 ft., stood beside the ancient Cathedral and must have been built in the time of Bishop Ursus, for, as it is clear that the Cathedral must have had its Baptistery from its very beginning, it is all the more probable that the building was erected during the first quarter of the 5th century. But the mosaic decoration is somewhat later: it goes back—according to the statement of Andrea-Agnello—to Bishop Neon whom we know to have occupied the episcopal throne of Ravenna a few years after the middle of the 5th century.

There are a few scholars (Bjvanck, Bettini) who think that the mosaics of the Baptistery are of the time of Ursus, but we do not share this opinion because the statement of Andrea-Agnello, author of the «Liber Pontificalis Ecclesiae Ravennatis», seems to us explicite, and we have no reason to doubt the words of the historian which run as follows: «Neon episcopus ...fontes Ursianae basilicae pulcherrime decoravit. Musiva et auratis tessellis Apostolorum imagines camera circumfixit» (Bishop Neon ...most beautifully adorned the Baptistery of the Ursian Basilica. He surrounded the figures of the Apostles with mosaics and gold tessellated work).

On account of the fact that an ancient inscription inside the Baptistery alluded to a change which had taken place in the building, some (Ricci, Gerola) have thought that originally it was simply a thermal establishment later transformed into the Baptistery, and all the more so because the first level was discovered nearly 10 ft. below the present one. But this supposition has now been rejected, also because Bettini has rightly observed that the original level of the Baptistery exactly corresponds to that of the early Cathedral near by.

The Baptistery has an octagonal form. Upon each of its sides there were originally alternately an apse and a door. The arches above the doors are still visible. The spacious interior is crowned by a cupola, but on the outside this is hidden by the walls of the octagon which support a roof. The upper part of the Baptistery was altered in a later age: Bettini thinks that the alteration took place in the 7th century, because the uprights of the part above suggest the period of the Exarchs, all the more as the roof was crowned with a Cross which was without doubt placed there in the days of Archbishop Theodore (677-691). Gerola is more disposed to see, in the uprights grouped together to form a pensile arch, a characteristic of late Byzantine architecture which almost amounts to an anticipation of the Romanesque, and as a result he is led to believe that this feature belongs to a period later than the 7th century. Galassi has even suggested the 10th century, for, in the series of small arches above, he has thought to see, not a point of departure but the conclusion of a long period of elaboration.

In order to explain the fact that the mosaic decoration is some decades later than the building of the Baptistery itself, Gerola has rightly considered that the original building consisted of an octagon covered with modern beams, and that it was Bishop Neon who raised below it the cupola which rests its weight partly on the eight arches of the zone containing the windows, and then, through the corner columns, upon the corresponding eight arches below. The fact that these lower arches back on to the wall of the octagon, and as a result, overlap the marble decoration, has given rise to the idea that this marble decoration («opus sectile») belongs to the early building. That seems likely enough, even if

The Baptistery of the Catholic Cathedral: Detail of the mosaic decoration of the dome

one scholar (Sas-Zaloziecky) has recently advanced the theory that it is the work of Archbishop Maximian (546-566).

However this may be, it is certain that the interior decoration of the Baptistery, with its calculated but just alternation of polished marble surfaces, stuccos and mosaics, is so intimately bound up with the architectural structure, that all the elements blend most admirably together, so that the building as a whole attains the highest degree of unity and harmony.

The lower mosaics which adorn the great arches of the lower zone have been much restored, because, during the last century, it was necessary to take steps to consolidate the wall below. The mosaic, which includes some small *male figures*, here consists of tapering *trails of green acanthus* sparkling with gold on a dark blue background. The colours are all the same as those in the mosaics of the so-called Mausoleum of Galla Placidia: an affinity which has given rise to the idea—even among those who attributed the mosaics of the cupola to Bishop Ursus—that this part of the ornamentation is due to Bishop Neon (Bettini).

The zone above this, containing the windows, is entirely adorned with stuccos. Beneath the curve of each of the great arches which support the cupola may be noted a rhythmical grouping of three minor arches, the central one, slightly wider, encloses the single window, while those at the side form niches in which are placed male figures (perhaps representing Old Testament *Prophets*) each holding a book in his hands. These stuccos, which still bear traces of colour, must at one time have still better performed the function of providing an adequate chromatic link between the mosaics of the lower zone and those of the upper. There is very little plastic vigour in these stucco figures, they appear somewhat flat, the better also to adapt themselves to the decoration as a whole, which is of exquisitely pictorial character.

It has been said that these stuccos were modelled by the same artists as those who carried out the mosaics (Tea), but Ricci has pointed out that this opinion is not acceptable, since the proportions of the figures in the mosaics are very different from those

The Baptistery of the Catholic Cathedral: Detail of the mosaic decoration of the dome

in the stucco. It is well known that a study of the proportions of an artist's figures yields one of the most reliable data in determining his characteristics.

Above this zone, which is covered with elaborate stuccos, rises the great cupola. Structurally this is formed by a double series of concentric rings overlapping one another, and is made of numerous little earthenware pipes which fit into one another. We see here the survival of the Roman tradition where a similar system had been adopted—the object being to make the cupola as light as possible and so reduce the lateral pressure determined by the vaulting. At its summit, however, the cupola is not covered with these earthenware tubes—as that of S. Vitale is—but instead by the lightest possible blocks of pumice.

The mosaic decoration of the cupola is divided into three zones, the medallion at the top being surrounded by two wide concentric bands.

The central disc shows the scene best adapted to the functions of a Baptistery: that of the *Baptism of Christ*. The Saviour is half immersed in the transparent blue-white waters of the river Jordan. From these same waters on the right side issues the personification of the river, a bearded figure carrying in his left hand a green rush—a common attribute of aquatic divinities in classical art—and in his right he holds a cloth, which, after the baptism, will be used to dry the Lord's body. On the left St. John the Baptist stands upright on the river banks, and is now seen with his right hand sustaining a «patera», or plate, halfway between the head of Jesus and the Dove symbolising the Holy Spirit. But this attitude was not in the original picture; it is due to restoration carried out—not in the 14th or 15th century as has been said (Strzygowsky)—but in the second half of last century by the Roman Felice Kibel. The area of restoration is clearly shown by the use of «tesserae» of a paler colour: it includes the Dove, the head of Christ, the upper part of the Cross, and also the head and right arm of the Baptist with the «patera». The original mosaic must have shown the Dove, but the hand of the Forerunner must have rested, without the «patera», directly on Christ's head, as is the case in similar representations, and, above all—to mention a mosaic in Ravenna itself—in the one still perfectly preserved in the Arian Baptistery, which is only a few decades later. The green cloth in the hand of the Jordan was not altered during the Renaissance as has been said (Heisenberg); it is certainly part of the original work and has never been retouched.

The band encircling the central disc contains figures of the *Twelve Apostles*: these, divided into two groups under the guidance respectively of St. Peter and St. Paul, can be individually distinguished by the name written beside the heads; they are separated from one another by graceful floral uprights each springing from a tuft of acanthus. They are all in gold tessellated work, their slender stems stand out, like the Apostles, on a dark blue background, and the tremulous sparkle which results gives the impression of a slight inner vibration.

All the Apostles, though not connected with one another by any link of movement, advance slowly over the green ground, with identically the same step, identically the same cadence. Each carries a crown as a symbol of victory, in his veiled hands—a detail which the artist certainly took from the ceremonial of the Imperial Court. All of them wear tunics and cloaks alternately white and gold. This alternation of vibrant notes of colour is well adapted to the animated colour scheme of the whole composition, and at the same time gives the opportunity of emphasizing a continuity of movement such as to recall to mind the ceaseless turning of everlasting wheels, «sempiterne rote», which Dante attributed to the spheres. Moreover, the impression of this rotating movement is still further increased if one follows the rhythmic way in which the blue drapery veined with red surrounding the central medallion falls in festoons and descends like a conical halo behind the heads of the Apostles. The figures of the Apostles themselves are so varied and individual, so vigorously expressive that one feels certain that the artist who executed the work must have been acquainted with Roman methods of figure-drawing, for in their portraits the Roman artists did not care to wander into the idealistic or the abstract, but sought to reproduce the reality with all its unmistakable characteristics.

The outermost band is, as it were divided into eight sections by *acanthus plants.* The decoration consists of two elements repeated alternately: a kind of portico curving in the centre in a semicircular space where one sees a *throne* with a cushion on which stands a cross; an *altar* supported by four small columns, bearing the book of one of the four Gospels. But while the throne is flanked by *two groups of plants behind carved parapets*, the altar is flanked by *two seats standing before two small apses.*

These architectural motifs have been taken to be a synthetic representation of the basilica (Gerola), more especially the terminal part, i.e. the sanctuary (Bettini). The seats would then be those of the deacons and the throne that of the Bishop (Stern). Another (Bettini) has seen in the throne a symbol of Christ's divinity as it is not empty but surmounted by a Cross. It is indeed this repeated presence of the «solium regale» which leads one to think that this decoration is intended to allude to the «etimasia» i.e. the preparation of the throne mentioned in the Book of Revelation.

Cecchelli has more justly seen in these mosaics the «regia coeli» or heavenly Jerusalem, and in the empty chairs the thrones prepared for the elect: «in my Father's house are many mansions; and I go to prepare a place for you...».

Taken as a whole, the design of the cupola therefore suggests the idea that, by virtue of the Baptism of Christ, every individual reborn in grace, will be able to attain the reward already given to the Apostles, and so win eternal life.

With regard to the mosaic decoration considered as a whole, a theory has recently been expressed (Bettini) referring to the way in which it may have been conceived. It has been said that the two bands surrounding the central disc should not be regarded as designs standing by themselves, but are to be interpreted as elements coming one before the other so as to constitute, together with the scene of the Baptism, a single vision.

The Baptistery of the Cathedral - Big marble vase of the Roman age

In other words, one should here apply the perspective known as «Plotinic» or «Polar» i.e. «inverse» with regard to the eye of the spectator—a perspective of which a few examples can be met with the late art of antiquity—thus we should imagine the Baptism of Christ as having taken place in the centre of the ring of Apostles who should be considered as standing out on the background of those buildings which in their recesses have thrones and altars. All this would be possible because the perspective would not be based on principles of objectivity, would not be expressed in the normal way, according to which figures become smaller as they recede from the observer. Here the perspective would assume an «expressionistic» character; i.e. it would no longer correspond to the natural representation of things according to the physical relationship of distance, but rather to a representation determined by the position of the personage whose figure constitutes the centre of the artist's conception: in this case it would be that of Christ.

This is certainly an ingenious theory, but we must point out that the first difficulty in accepting it lies in the fact that the figure of Christ is not, as one would logically expect, larger than those of the Apostles, but is considerably smaller.

However this may be, what seems to us to be the most impressive characteristic of the mosaics of the Baptistery is the extraordinarily lively impression produced by the disposition of the various colours, which flash with all their brightness in the greatest variety of tones. We have blue, gold, red, green, sulphur-yellow, violet, azure sky-blue, white, grey etc. and many of these colours show the most varied gradations. Thus, for example, green is seen in all the tints which have for their basis emerald green, grass-green, mouldy-green, apple-green, olive-green, and so on—while the azure is at times deep, at other times pale, now it shows lights of lapis-lazuli, and now of cobalt, now it is transparent as sea-water, now dull and fading into grey.

Moreover, as our own eyes embrace the great mosaic in its entirety, we may notice how those of the spectator are drawn towards the scene enclosed in the medallion, but afterwards find no important decorative point on which to linger. Each individual element is in fact so closely and intimately bound to the rest of the structural whole, as to cooperate with it in the formation of an organic whole which also adapts itself splendidly to the circular form of the cupola, given the fact that the general scheme of the composition may be compared—as has already rightly been pointed out (A. Rossi)—to a great wheel with many spokes rotating around a fixed nucleus, i.e. the central medallion. For it is indeed due to the centrifugal force of this rotating movement that the decoration suggests the idea of the continuous and the indefinite, and that the vault appears to tend to become lower and wider.

The Archiepiscopal Museum: marble pulpit coming from St. John and Paul's church

THE ARCHIEPISCOPAL MUSEUM

Close to the Cathedral Baptistery stands the Archbishop's Palace. In 1955 part of an ancient wall with a double window («bifora») was found on its ground floor. On the first floor of the Palace there is a small but very interesting Museum.

The most striking object in the collection is without question the celebrated **Ivory Throne of Maximian.** This precious treasure is perhaps the most beautiful work in ivory which the ancient world has handed down to us. It is thought that this throne, a real flower of 6th century carving, was presented by the Emperor Justinian to the learned and ambitious Maximian of Pola who was consecrated Bishop of Ravenna on the 14th of October, 546. It seems moreover that the chair is the same one as that presented in December 1001 by the Doge of Venice, Pietro Orseolo II to the Emperor Otto III, who was then residing at Ravenna. The Emperor—according to the narrative of the «Cronaca Veneziana» by the deacon Giovanni—was very pleased with the gift, but at the same time, decided with true generosity that the precious object must always be kept at Ravenna.

The presence of the monogram «Maximianus episcopus» leaves no doubt that the throne was made towards the middle of the 6th century, before Maximian had assumed the title of «Archbishop». A minute analysis of its style has revealed that the decoration is not all the work of the same artist; there seem to have been four master-carvers. The first is thought to have executed the front of the seat showing *St. John the Baptist and the four Evangelists*; as the personages, set beneath arches and shown frontally, recall a scheme widely used in earlier Asiatic sculpture, the theory has been advanced that the artist responsible for this part was no stranger to Anatolian influences. To the second master, less highly gifted than the first, are due the panels with the *Gospel scenes* that adorn the back. These reliefs are not lacking in pictorial quality and in Hellenistic echoes, for which reason it has been thought that they are by an artist of the Alexandrian school. The third, to whose hand we owe the splendid series of panels along the sides of the chair showing episodes in the *life of the Hebrew Joseph,* must, it is thought, have been Egyptian. The scenes are full of animation, the carving deep and decided. To a fourth sculptor, who was certainly in contact with the Syrian tradition in art, are attributed the parts which may be more properly called decorative i.e. the many borders showing luxuriant vine trails within the coils of which are seen many animals. In this rich system of decoration an attempt has been made to create a strong effect of light and shade, and to bring into relief the eminently pictorial values of the work.

Notwithstanding these differences and these contrasting influences, the chair which some scholars think was made at Alexandria in Egypt (Cecchelli), and others at Constantinople (Bettini), forms one unitary and organic whole. This is due to the fact that in the 6th century the language of art still drove its roots into the «species mille» of that which was the «ars una» of the Roman world.

The Museum contains some *marble funeral pillars* (*stele*) *of the «classiarii»* or soldiers of the Roman fleet stationed at Classe, and some fragments of the Roman relief known as the *«throne of Neptune»*—two of which are still today inserted in the walls of the choir of S. Vitale—and the small ancient *Christian funeral pillar* attributed to the end of the 2nd or the beginning of the 3rd century (De Rossi). It was brought to light in one of the

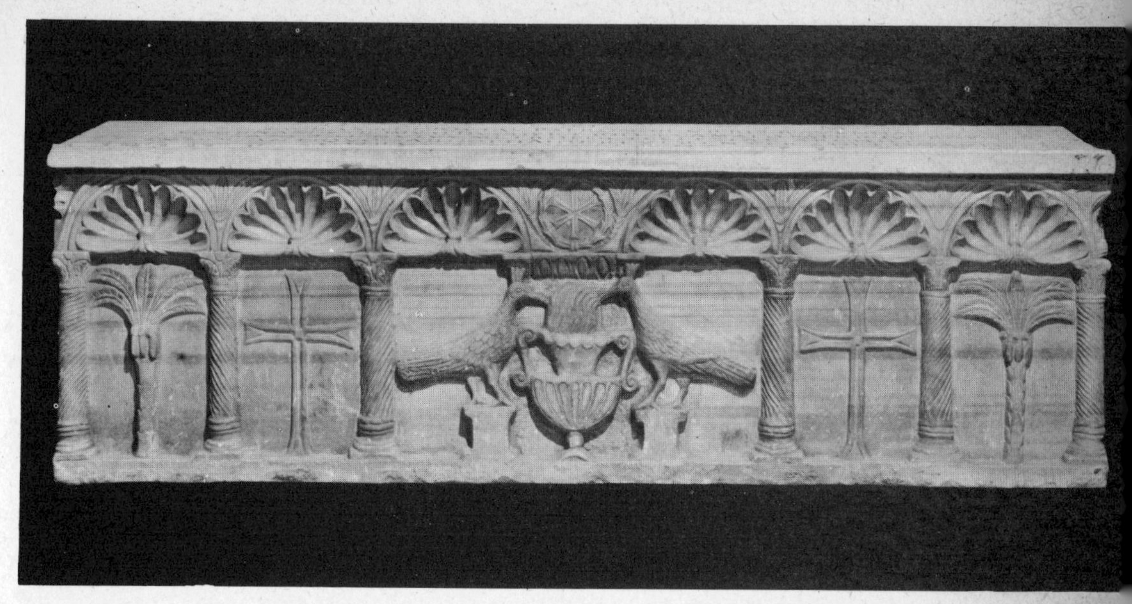

Sarcophagus

The Archiepiscopal Museum:
Marble chest with the scene of the Magi offering their gifts

early Christian cemeteries not far from S. Apollinare in Classe, and has the figure of the Good Shepherd on the upper part, while in the inscription below is mentioned a certain Antifonte who died at the age of 17 years, 5 months and 12 days.

Very fine is the *porphyry statue*, nearly 4 ft. high, representing an imperial personage. It is unfortunately headless; it was once thought that the porphyry head called that of Carmagnola in St. Mark's at Venice, might belong to this statue (Conway), but a test effected by means of a plaster cast has discredited this theory. Some scholars (Mendel, Delbrueck) think the statue at Ravenna may go back to the 4th century, while others (Bartoccini, S. Muratori) say to the 6th, and that it might represent the Emperor Justinian.

The small *marble chest* formerly set in the wall of the campanile of St. John the Baptist, belongs to the second half of the 5th century. On its four sides it shows: Daniel in the Lions' den, the Adoration of the Magi, the Holy Women at the Sepulchre and the Ascension of Jesus, and the «Traditio Legis», or appointment of St. Peter to the government of the Church.

Interesting also are *four capitals*; two of them show acanthus leaves in the lower part, and in the upper part various animals (rams, eagles etc.) while the other two have a vine trail in openwork below, and above four eagles alternating with the heads of an ox and a lion. It has been said that these capitals come from the ancient Ursian Cathedral (Ricci), but now this is considered doubtful. Some think them to be of the first decades of the 5th century (Strzygowski), while others (Cecchelli) refer them to the 6th.

To the age of Theodoric must be assigned the *two capitals* that bear the monogram of Bishop Petrus with the symbols of the Evangelists surmounting acanthus leaves which seem to be stirred by the wind.

From the Ursian Basilica come some «transenne», or large carved panels, which may originally have been intended to enclose the «schola cantorum». They go back to about the middle of the 6th century.

Ivory throne of Maximian

To the end of the 6th century—as is proved by the inscription mentioning Bishop Marinianus—is the *part of the marble pulpit* from the church of Saints John and Paul. In its shape and in the disposition of the decorative elements which consist of a series of animals within small panels, and in the flatness of its relief, it closely resembles the pulpit preserved in the Cathedral.

The *fragments of mosaic* attached to the walls i.e. those showing the Virgin in attitude of prayer, and the heads of the Saints John the Evangelist, Peter, Barbatianus, Ursicinus, and a soldier, are all that remains of the great decoration executed in mosaic in 1112 in the apse of the Ursian Basilica which was demolished in the first half of the 18th century.

To the last years of the 7th century, or the early 8th have been attributed (Mazzotti) certain *stuffs* found in 1949 in some sarcophagi of S. Apollinare in Classe: especially worthy of note is the purple silk veil, while some fragments of episcopal belts with uncial inscriptions are important and well preserved.

There is also a splendid chasuble in dark blue brocade, bearing as decorative motifs figures of eagles and small moons; it is usually called the *chasuble of Angeloptes.* It is attributed to the second half of the 12th century (Braun).

THE ARCHBISHOP'S CHAPEL

On the same floor as the Museum is the Archbishop's Chapel, also called the Oratory of S. Andrea, which is reached by passing along a short corridor. The Chapel was built by Bishop Petrus II who occupied the episcopal throne during the reign of Theodoric, from 494 to 519.

The Chapel proper is preceded by a rectangular vestibule with barrel-vaulting. This vaulting is covered with ornamental mosaic on a background of gold which shows various retouchings and completions in tempera. The decorative motif is substantially given by the crossing of white lily flowers which enclose within the space thus formed, the most varied birds and animals, among which may be recognised doves, partridges, parrots, peacocks, ducks and guinea-fowl.

Along the walls we see, reproduced in tempera in imitation of mosaic, twenty Latin hexameters, which were once read and annotated by the historian Andrea-Agnello. A few traces of them in mosaic were discovered by Gerola who could consequently make out the complete transcription in painting. The first verse of this long inscription—from reading which we gather that the Chapel was used for the custody of relics and for the sacrament of confession—is truly magnificent. Above all it emphasises the essential characteristic of mosaic, which is to exalt, by the precious material of which it is composed, the luminous elements of colour. In fact the verse, which runs as follows: «Aut lux hic nata est aut capta hic libera regnat», means «Either light was born here, or, made captive, here reigns in freedom».

Above the door of the vestibule there is a lunette with the figure of *Christus militans*, but from the middle of the bust downward it is all restored. The Christ must originally also have rested his feet on a lion and a serpent, because a few small remains of these have been found. The Saviour, with head surrounded by a halo marked with a cross, wears a breastplate and a purple mantle. He is seen full-face, and while he carries a cross on his right shoulder, with his left hand he holds an open book, on the page of which are written the words: «Ego sum via, veritas et vita» (I am the way, the truth and the life). This portrayal of Christ as a warrior trampling—as one of the Psalms says—on the lion and the dragon, is not new in the art of Ravenna. It had been represented, for example, several decades earlier in one of those precious and well-preserved stuccos in the Cathedral Baptistery.

Through a door which opens in the centre of one of the walls of the vestibule, we enter the little Oratory itself. It has the form of a Greek Cross which ends in a small apse facing the entrance. It has cross-vaulting and is completely covered with mosaic. Along the ascending lines of the triangles we see *four Angels* clad in white and supporting with raised arms a disc bearing the letters I and X, initials in Greek of the name of Jesus Christ.

In the midst of these white figures of Angels who stand out on the gold expanse of background, are seen emerging from clouds bright with many colours, the *winged symbols of the Evangelists*, among which that of St. Matthew is especially deserving of mention.

The intrados, or underside, of the four arches which support the vaulting are all adorned with *figures within medallions*.

In the east and west arches, the intrados has at its sum-

IACO BVS
PAV LVS
PET RVS
AND REAS

Cappella Arcivescovile: interno dell'oratorio
Archiepiscopal Chapel: interior of the oratory

Vault of the Archbishop's Chapel

Vestibule of the Archbishop's Chapel: the Redeemer

XIIth cent. mosaic from the Cathedral church

mit the *bust of Christ* flanked by *busts of the Apostles*, six on each side. The youthful countenance of Christ in these two medallions shows the closest affinity with that of the warrior Christ; considering this fact, it has been rightly observed (Muñoz) that both in the vestibule and in the Chapel the mosaic was the work of one and the same master.

On the intrados of the south and the north arches we see respectively the busts of *six male Saints* (partially restored) and *six female Saints*. Their faces wear an expression of gravity and austerity which is concentrated above all in their fixed motionless glance, and even in the case of the female Saints this is not relieved by the white veils which fall over their hair adorned with many gems.

The semidome of the apse has been entirely worked over with imitation mosaic painted in tempera to represent the night sky lit up with stars. In these latter Gerola was able to trace some minute remains of the original work. Structurally the vault of the apse—as discoveries on the spot have proved—was carried out by using small earthenware tubes, as in other examples of the same kind.

From the author of the «Liber Pontificalis Ecclesiae Ravennatis» we learn that the lunette above the entrance once contained the portrait of Bishop Petrus, founder of the Chapel. The south and north lunettes were also adorned with mosaics: in the latter, which was decorated in the 16th century with a fresco by Longhi, we can still perceive the traces of some tesserae, which, small though the remains are, have made possible the conclusion that they formed part of a scene with green earth and a background of gold.

Upon a marble slab on the east side (in the corner near the window) there are some graffiti: one is in memory of Archbishop Enrico (1052-1072): «Dominus Enricus Archiepis», and another advises us to shun the man who drinks no wine: «Vitamus d(ominum) q(ui) vino n(on) pote(st) bibere».

MUNICIPAL PICTURE GALLERY

(PINACOTECA CIVICA)

This Gallery is to be found on the first floor of the Accademia di Belle Arti (Academy of the Fine Arts) in a building, which, though of very simple form, bears the stamp of a classical harmony. The Pinacoteca or Gallery was founded by Ignazio Sarti of Bologna in 1827; the present arrangement is of a temporary character.

The paintings which constitute the most important group are those of the school of Romagna; we limit ourselves here to pointing out those which are most representative. Niccolò Rondinelli, the greatest of Ravenna's painters of the Renaissance period and a follower of Giovanni Bellini, attains in his works expression pervaded by a gentle melancholy, as can be seen, for example, in his *Madonna crowned by two Angels, between St. Catherine and St. Jerome.* Francesco Zaganelli of Cotignola shows the spirit of an innovator in the composition of some of his pictures, as one may notice in his *Adoration of the Shepherds*, even if an archaic background of gold lies behind his figures. Luca Longhi, whose mind was open to the most varied influences, but who was often very mannered, shows the greatest vigour in his portraits, such as those of the physician *Giovanni Arrigoni,* and the captain *Raffaele Rasponi.*

The collection is valuable also for many other pictures by painters of other schools and other tendencies like Guercino (*S. Romualdo*), Palmezzano (*Nativity,* the *Presentation in the Tem-*

ple), Ludovico Carracci (*Head of Christ*), Lorenzo Monaco (*Crucifixion*), Niccolò Alunno (*Christ with the Cross between two Angels*), and others. The floor of one large room consists of a great Roman mosaic discovered in 1875 near the Church of S. Apollinare in Classe: it is worthy of mention because the grace of the ornamental motifs is combined with a delicate harmony in the colours.

In a small separate room, the further end of which shows 16th century panelling, is to be seen the recumbent figure of *Guidarello Guidarelli,* one of Duke Valentine's men-at-arms, who was killed at Imola for petty motives in 1501 by a certain Virgilio Romano. The statue is the work of Tullio Lombardo, and was commissioned by the dead man's widow in 1525, when it was placed in one of the chapels of the Church of St. Francis. The contrast is very remarkable between the soft modelling of the face and the unyielding hardness of the armour which clothes the entire body. «La vita della morte» (G. Capponi)—the life of death—shines from this young knight's face where the lines express indefinable suffering, as D'Annunzio has written in his «Laudi»: *dorme supino con le man conserte su la spada sua grande. Al volto inerte ferro, morte, dolor furon suggello.*

(He sleeps with hands clasped on his great sword. On his lifeless face iron, death and pain have set their seal).

Tullio Lombardo: Guidarello Guidarelli

The Municipal Picture Gallery - Antonio Vivarini: The Crucifixion

S. Francesco

CHURCH OF SAN FRANCESCO

This church was originally dedicated to the Apostles, but of the early building which the historian Andrea-Agnello declares to have been erected by Bishop Neon—therefore about the middle of the 5th century—only a few remains have survived and these are now below the ground. The mosaic decoration which must have adorned the semidome of the apse has also completely disappeared. It represented—to quote the «Liber Pontificalis Ecclesiae Ravennatis»—the Apostles Peter and Paul beside a Cross with the inscription below: «Domnus Neon Episcopus senescat nobis».

What the plan and proportions of this early «Apostoleion» were we have no means of knowing: Gerola thinks they were different from those of the present church, which, as we now see it, is merely a reconstruction carried out in the 10th and 11th centuries. On the other hand the square **tower**, about 108 ft. high—the upper part of which has been raised—is a little earlier than the reconstructed church. It is to be attributed, not so much to the 8th century as has been said (Galassi), but to the end of the 9th (Gerola, Ricci).

The church was also called that of S. Pier Maggiore, but when, in 1261, it was granted to the Conventual Friars of St. Francis, these latter gave it the name of S. Francesco which it still retains. In 1321 the funeral rites of Dante Alighieri were celebrated in this church, and his body was laid in an ancient sarcophagus near the portico.

The **interior** of the church (about 152 ft. by 77 ft.), in the simplicity, not to say bareness, of its architectural lines, leaves a profound impression. It has a nave and two aisles and two fine rows of columns of veined Greek marble, surmounted by the original «pulvini» and by capitals the leaves of which have recently been almost all worked over in order to remedy the chiselling which they underwent during the alterations of 1793.

The fine ceiling that looks like the overturned keel of a ship—formerly hidden by a covering of basketwork and plaster—was restored to its original form in 1921, with the help of old fragments.

It is to be noted that the last two columns of the central nave—one on the right and the other on the left—are on a level more than 5 ft. lower than the others. These latter in fact, as is the case in other churches in Ravenna—have been raised to their higher level because of the steady rise of water in the ground below.

A **crypt**, like an oratory, supported by several columns lies below the apse, but it is now filled with water. It goes back to a time shortly before the year 1000. In the course of certain investigations, some mosaic pavings with Greek and Latin inscriptions were found beneath its present level. It is very likely that one of these epigraphs refers to the first tomb of Bishop Neon.

In 1920, at the further end of the left aisle, some *14th century frescoes* were discovered. They have been variously attributed to Giovanni Baronzio (Ricci), and to Pietro da Rimini or his school (Toesca).

Among the various *marble sarcophagi* preserved in the church two are especially worthy of attention: the one half way along the left aisle, and the one which supports the mensa of the High Altar. They are both of the 5th century and show in very fine workmanship Christ and the Apostles within niches flanked by small columns generally spiral in form.

Church of San Francesco (Interior)

Dante's Tomb

THE TOMB OF DANTE

Not far from the left side of the church of St. Francis stands Dante's tomb. Its form is that of a small temple erected in 1780 by the architect Camillo Morigia, by order of the Cardinal Legate Luigi Valenti Gonzaga, whose coat-of-arms is seen above the door. The lintel bears the inscription «Dantis poetae sepulcrum». The exterior of this mausoleum is in the Neoclassical style, and though its lines are sober and graceful, it is a very modest building when one remembers that its interior, even if panelled with marble, guards the bones of the loftiest of poets. Here, upon the further wall, is the famous Latin epitaph composed in 1357 by Bernardo Canaccio:

IURA MONARCHIAE SUPEROS PHLEGETONTA LACUSQUE
LUSTRANDO CECINI VOLVERUNT FATA QUOUSQUE;
SED QUIA PARS CESSIT MELIORIBUS HOSPITA CASTRIS
AUCTOREMQUE SUUM PETIIT FELICIOR ASTRIS,
HIC CLAUDOR DANTES PATRIIS EXTORRIS AB ORIS
QUEM GENUIT PARVI FLORENTIA MATER AMORIS.

(«The rights of monarchy, when visiting the skies and waters of Phlegethon, I sang as long as my mortal life endured. But since my soul departed to dwell in better regions, and more blessed still, reached its Creator among the stars, here I, Dante, lie enclosed, an exile from the country that gave me birth, Florence, a mother too little loving»).

In the centre of the temple a votive lamp hangs from the summit of the cupola; it is fed with oil from the Tuscan hills sent every year by the municipal government of Florence on the anniversary of the poet's death.

But Dante's bones have not always rested here. In fact, the great poet died during the night of September 13th, 1321, and after the solemn funeral celebrated in the church of St. Francis, his body was laid in an ancient sarcophagus near the portico of the church. Towards the end of the 15th century, the Venetian Podestà of Ravenna, Bernardo Bembo, moved the sepulchre and placed it so that it backed on the wall of one of those peaceful and harmonious cloisters (recently restored) of the monastery of St. Francis.

In 1519 Pope Leo X, a member of the Medici family, in response to a petition signed among others by Michelangelo Buonarroti, granted permission to the Florentines to transfer Dante's bones to Florence. But the friars of the church, learning of this, and desiring to preserve the precious remains for the city of Ravenna, made a breach in the cloister wall behind the tomb, and removed the poet's bones which they guarded jealously in their monastery; now and then a verification took place, the most noted being that carried out in 1677 by P. Antonio Santi.

After a long concealment, the bones were at last re-discovered in 1865 in a neighbouring garden, beside the fourfold arch of Braccioforte, beneath which are preserved some ancient marble sarcophagi, the most celebrated of which is very fitly the one belonging to the beginning of the 5th century, and bearing various scenes mentioned by Gabriele d'Annunzio in his «Francesca da Rimini»:

Interior of the Tomb of Dante

il Redentore
ha sotto i piedi il leone e la serpe;
Elisabetta visita Maria;
l'Annunciatore appare a Nostra Donna;
i cervi si dissetano alla fonte.

(The Redeemer has beneath his feet the lion and the serpent; Elizabeth visits Mary; The Announcing Angel appears to Our Lady; the stags quench their thirst at the spring).

One of the Cloisters of the ex-convent of St. Francis

PIAZZA MAGGIORE

(PIAZZA DEL POPOLO)

This extensive piazza is rectangular in form, and is the true centre of the city. It is bordered by several public buildings—the Palazzo Comunale (Town Hall), the Palazzetto Veneziano, the Palazzo della Prefettura and the Palazzo dell'Orologio.

The most ancient and impressive part is the south-west corner where the Town Hall makes an angle with the Palazzetto Veneziano to which it is united by a bridge over the street.

The **Palazzo Comunale** (Town Hall) has a façade divided into three parts; in front of the lower part there is a portico with wide but somewhat low arches. In the one above we see five corniced windows, the middle one opening on a balcony; in the third or upper one, edged above by a massive cornice of brickwork above which are heavy battlements constructed towards the middle of the last century, are five round windows. The Palace was almost entirely rebuilt in 1681, and certain additions were made to it in the last century.

The **Palazzetto Veneziano**—built at the end of the 15th century—also has an airy portico in front of it, but above this there is a single floor which is gracefully adorned by several double windows («bifore») and a small balcony. The strong granite columns of the portico are surmounted by capitals decorated with acanthus leaves which appear blown out by the wind;

they show on all sides dense open-work achieved by trepanning. They were used in this building by the Venetians after having been brought from the church of S. Andrea dei Goti. Four of them bear the monogram «Theodericus Rex», like others now to be seen in the National Museum.

In 1483 the Venetians placed two lofty **columns** in front of the Palazzo Comunale, upon one stood the statue of St. Apollinaris (first Bishop of Ravenna) and on the other the Lion of St. Mark. The latter was taken down in 1509 when Ravenna returned to the Church, its place being taken by a statue of St. Vitalis. Very striking are the circular bases of the columns with steps running round them on which Pietro Lombardi carved graceful ornamental designs.

Piazza Maggiore

CHURCH OF SAN GIOVANNI EVANGELISTA

In spite of some alterations brought about during the course of the centuries, and in spite of the severe damage caused by an air raid in 1944, this church on the whole retains its original architectural appearance. The atrium which was once in front of it no longer exists, but a lofty mediaeval porch projects in a striking manner adorning the brick façade, while beside it stands the massive square **Campanile** (139 ft. high) from the summit of which issues the sad, mournful sound, as a pious legend says, of the two bells cast in 1208 by a certain Robertus de Sasono.

The sacred building was begun by the Empress Galla Placidia in fulfilment of a vow she made during the dangerous voyage from Constantinople to Ravenna in order to assume the government of the Western Empire for her young son Valentinian III.

Shortly after its erection the church was enlarged so as to take in the space originally intended for the narthex. One can notice signs of this in the double arch to be seen along the side walls as soon as one has crossed the threshold.

The **interior** (163 ft. by 73 ft.) is wide and well lighted and is divided into a central nave and two aisles by two rows of columns which have been raised about 5 ft. above the level of the original pavement.

The choir arch and the semidome of the apse are now covered with simple white plaster, but from the 5th to the 16th century they were brilliant with mosaics of the greatest interest —for they comprised portraits of almost all the members of the family of Theodosius, and twice over a representation of the scene of how St. John the Evangelist saved from destruction the ship in which Galla Placidia was sailing with her children.

The apse, which is semicircular on the inside and polygonal on the outside, is not only, as is usually the case, flanked by the two typical rectangular chapels known as the «diaconicon» and the «prothesis», but shows an unusual feature in that continuous series of seven openings, which, supported by elegant marble columns, has the appearance of a loggia. Below this can be seen the outlines of three windows that are now closed. According to some scholars (Ricci, Gerola, Rivoira, Giovannoni) these three windows were closed while the work was still in progress, because of a sudden change in the original plan; according to others (Bettini), the three lower windows and the seven windows higher up, were of the 5th century—with the difference that the former were originally intended to give light, while the others were blind and merely had a decorative value for the exterior. Others again have rejected these theories and have thought that the loggia was opened only on the exterior considerably later, in the 8th century (Galassi) or during the 11th or 12th (Cecchelli).

The fragments of mosaic arranged along the walls came from the various pavements which at different levels (and therefore in various periods) adorned the church. Together with some sections of mosaic belonging to the most ancient pavements, are to be seen various panels of mosaic made in 1213 by order of the Abbot Guglielmo; they show simple popular subjects, fantastic animals, a fox's funeral, and episodes seeming to refer to the Fourth Crusade, as one concludes from representations of the taking of Zara and of Constantinople.

In the chapel opening about half way along the left aisle are the remains of some 14th century frescoes. Those on the vaulting show the *Four Evangelists*, each with his symbol, and

S. Giovanni Evangelista - The apse and the North side

S. Giovanni Evangelista

S. Giovanni Evangelista - The Gothic portal

the *Doctors of the Church*: St. Jerome, St. Ambrose, St. Augustine and St. Gregory. Some critics have attributed them to Giotto (Ricci), others with greater probability, to Giovanni Baronzio da Rimini (L. Venturi).

Mosaic fragment of the ancient pavement representing the taking of Costantinople by the Crusaders (13th century)

Mosaic fragment of the ancient pavement representing a fox's funeral (13th century)

THE CHURCH OF SPIRITO SANTO

Like the ancient Catholic Cathedral, the Arian Cathedral —now the Church of Spirito Santo—was originally dedicated to the «Aghìa Anastasis», i.e. the Resurrection of the Lord. It was built by King Theodoric and it is very probable that the building arose at the end of the 5th century, i.e. in the years immediately following the Gothic King's entry into Ravenna (493), since it may be supposed that Theodoric was anxious at once to give his people who were Arians, churches of their own, so that they need not have been obliged to use Catholic churches.

The apse must at first have been adorned with mosaics, for we know that in the restorations of 1853 traces of these were found, while «many tesserae a few centimetres below the paving of the apse itself (Ricci) were also discovered. The original floor of the church lies considerably below the level of the present one, as can easily be gathered from the arched tops of the ancient doors which can be seen on the inner wall of the façade.

The marble *pulpit*, about half way up the row of columns on the right, also goes back to the age of Theodoric.

After the expulsion of the Goths in 540 and during the episcopate of Agnellus (556-569) the church passed into the hands of the Catholics, and was dedicated first to St. Theodore and then to the Holy Spirit.

In the **interior** of this ample and well lighted church two things should be noticed: first, at the beginning of the left aisle, an ancient *marble sarcophagus* which was, in the 17th century, used as a sepulchre by the noble Pasolini family (as one assumes from the presence on it of their coat-of-arms); secondly, at the end of the right aisle the large painting by Livio Agresti of Forlì, portraying the «*Colombini Bishops*» who were thus called because their election was believed to be due to the Dove (= colomba) which symbolises the Holy Spirit.

The graceful **portico** in front of the church seems to go back to the 16th century. It is supported by five columns and three semicolumns of Greek marble. These latter, spiral in their upper part before being sawn across, had once been part of the ancient altar-canopy of the church.

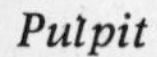

Pulpit

THE ARIAN BAPTISTERY

This is a somewhat small building of octagonal shape with four apses. Originally it was surrounded on seven sides by an ambulatory, and between 1915 and 1918 Gerola discovered part of its foundations.

It is not known exactly when this Baptistery was erected. We can only say that it arose in the days of Theodoric and assume that it was built as soon as the neighbouring Arian Cathedral was finished, i.e. towards the end of the 5th century.

A simple glance at the mosaic decoration of the cupola—which is constructed in brick and not with earthenware tubes—convinces the spectator that the artist who planned it took his idea from the decoration of the cupola of the Cathedral Baptistery, because the composition shows almost the same geometrical arrangement of the parts. There is however some difference: what strikes the eye is not so much the greater bareness of the interior (for we must imagine that the early Baptistery was richly adorned all along the side walls with frescoes and mosaics) as that the medallion in the centre is not surrounded by two concentric bands, but by one only. This was determined by the smaller size of the building which called for a cupola with a shorter diameter.

In the central medallion we see the *Baptism of Christ*. Only three persons are represented there, as in that of Bishop Neon's Baptistery, but the artist did not wish to follow his model too closely, for though he placed in the centre the figure of the Redeemer immersed deeply in the water, he puts the Baptist, not on his right hand, but on his left, and the River Jordan—whose head here is adorned with a lobster's pincers—is not seen emerging from the waters he personifies, but is seated on Christ's right hand against a vase from which the water flows.

Another difference from the design in the Cathedral Baptistery is seen in the band surrounding the central disc which is encircled by a sort of garland. In this band again we see the *Twelve Apostles*, and here too they are in two distinct groups, led, one by St. Peter, the other by St. Paul. They meet before a great *throne surmounted by a Cross.*

The plan of placing a throne in the band with the procession of the Apostles, and so maintaining the same meaning and the allusion to the «etimasia» of the decoration of the Cathedral Baptistery was a really brilliant idea, but the same cannot be said of the fact that the meeting of the two Princes of the Apostles is not in symmetry with the scene of Baptism; indeed, to obtain a good view of St. Peter and St. Paul at the sides of the throne, the spectator must take his stand on the side exactly opposite that from which he can best admire the Baptismal scene.

The Apostles all have the halo, but their names are not written beside their heads; they advance slowly over the grass with the same cadence and are separated one from another by slender palm branches. In their hands they each carry a crown of victory, but St. Peter holds the keys and St. Paul a rolled up scroll.

It has been said (Galassi) that the medallion with the scene of the Baptism is almost two centuries later than the band with the Apostles. But it has been proved beyond doubt by studies of a technical character (Ricci, Bartoccini) that this is not the case; we can only say that several artists worked at this mosaic; the Apostles, for example, reveal the hand of more than one mosaicist.

Battistero degli Ariani: La Cupola

Baptistery of the Arians: The Cupola

The Arian Baptistery

On the other hand, when the real property of the Arians passed into the possession of the Catholics, the Baptistery was transformed into the church of S. Maria in Cosmedin shortly after the middle of the 6th century. It is thus obvious that if the central medallion had been altered afterwards the scene would certainly not have been that of the Baptism, but, as the church had been dedicated to the Madonna, it would have been adorned with a figure of the Virgin.

Mosaics of the cupola

S. Apollinare Nuovo: La chiamata di Pietro e di Andrea (particolare)

S. Apollinare Nuovo: The call of Peter and Andrew (detail)

SANT'APOLLINARE NUOVO

The Basilica now called by the name of S. Apollinare Nuovo was originally an Arian church. It was built by Theodoric who dedicated it to the Redeemer. This is definitely stated by a passage in the «Liber Pontificalis Ecclesiae Ravennatis», in which the historian Andrea-Agnello, quoted the inscription which ran upon a band above the windows of the apse: «Theodericus Rex hanc ecclesiam a fundamentis in nomine Domini nostri Jesu Christi fecit» (King Theodoric built this church from its foundations in the name of Our Lord Jesus Christ).

There is thus no doubt that the building of the Basilica must be assigned to the period between 493 when the Goths entered Ravenna, and 526 when Theodoric died.

But it was not for long that the sacred edifice remained in Arian hands, for after Ravenna had been taken by the Byzantines, Archbishop Agnellus, between 556 and 565, consecrated the church for Catholic use after the edict issued by the Emperor Justinian giving to the «Sancta Mater Ecclesia Ravennae, vera Mater orthodoxa» all the property formerly belonging to the Arians. After this «reconciliation» the church was dedicated to St. Martin, the famous Bishop who had fought against the heretics so vigorously as to be considered one of their bitterest foes, and to have earned for himself the title of «Malleus Haereticorum»

(Hammer of the heretics). It is thus obvious that a definite and deliberate intention animated Archbishop Agnellus in his choice of a Saint to whom to dedicate the basilica where once the Arian heretics had officiated.

But the name of St. Martin was also destined to fall into oblivion. This happened towards the middle of the 9th century, when, to save the sacred relics of St. Apollinaris, Ravenna's first Bishop, from the danger of profanation in one of the piratical invasions at the time frequent along the Adriatic coasts, it was decided to transfer—or to appear to transfer—the venerated bones of the saint from the splendid church at Classe to that of St. Martin which would be much safer because of its position within the walls of the city.

It was from this time that the church was usually called S. Apollinare, but with the addition still retained of «Nuovo» or «In Novo» (new). This does not imply any distinction of chronological character between this church and S. Apollinare in Classe (which was built a few decades later than the Arian church) but is intended to distinguish it from another of the city churches of the same name, but certainly smaller and more ancient, called «ad Monetam Veterem» and also «in Veclo».

At one time there seems to have been an atrium before the façade of the church, which has been altered several times during the centuries. Today there is a simple and elegant portico with round arches, which was rebuilt in the 16th century. To the right stands a slender round *Campanile* more than 125 ft. high. It has windows with a single opening, others with two openings («bifore») and again others with three («trifore»), and these help to relieve the solidity of the building which thus acquires an appearance of much greater lightness.

The **interior** of the church (about 138 ft. by 69 ft.) is divided into a central nave with two aisles by a double row of columns, 12 on each side. They are of Greek marble, and Greek ciphers and letters which are often repeated in different capitals, are often carved on them. They are evidently identification marks

S. Apollinare Nuovo

of the oriental work-shops in which the marbles were prepared. The capitals, all of corinthian type, are surmounted by «pulvini» which serve to separate the walls above still further from the columns.

The present paving is about 4 ft. above the level of the original floor. The columns were all brought to their present level at the beginning of the 16th century, and as a result all the arches were lifted, to the detriment of one section of the wall, i.e. that which was originally between the cornice from which the mosaic decoration starts, and the line given by the upper part of the pulvini. It may be that in this lost part there was a decoration—not of inlaid marble (Rohault de Fleury) or of mosaic (Ricci) but of stuccos: these latter, in fact, are mentioned with satisfaction in Andrea-Agnello's «Liber Pontificalis».

The apse at the further end of the church was rebuilt in 1950. It was raised on the very walls of the ancient building which were brought to light in that same year. The original apse was semicircular on the inside and pentagonal on the outside.

Before 1950 the church ended in a very deep baroque apse. Though damaged during the war it was still left standing in spite of the erection of the present apse. While the work for the erection of the new apse was in progress, the crypt below the choir was explored. As it is always filled with water it can no longer be visited. Its form is that of a semianular ambulatory with barrel vaulting, to the centre of which is added a rectilineal corridor. It is of a type characteristic of the 9th century, but its erection must belong to the time of the actual or presumed transference of the bones of St. Apollinaris from the church at Classe outside the walls to this church.

While the earth was being removed from the outer walls in 1950 some small terracotta tubes pointed at one end were brought to light. Here we have the usual light material used in Ravenna for the construction of the domes of churches and apses; it is therefore not unreasonable to suppose that the dome of S. Apollinare Nuovo—which was gravely damaged by an earthquake in

Basilica di S. Apollinare Nuovo: Il corteo delle Sante (particolare)

Basilica of Sant'Apollinare Nuovo: detail of the Saints

The mosaic decoration of the South wall

The mosaic decoration of the North wall

the days of Archbishop Giovanni V—was originally made of this special building material.

Close to the steps which lead from the central nave to the raised choir are placed three «*transenne*» i.e. large carved marble panels, and a pluteus, all these sculptures save one may be assigned to the 6th century and by their carved open-work, determined by the alternation of mass and space—and therefore of light and shade—they produce the typical black and white appearance which adds so greatly to their pictorial character.

The «*pluteus*», which is the first sculpture we meet on the left, shows on its front a vase from which spring two peacocks facing the monogrammatic cross between. Until 1950 it was inset in the wall of one of the chapels of the church; it was then removed in order to be given a more conspicuous position, and, for the first time, the ornamentation on the back was revealed. The decorative design unites here with a Biblical scene. Amid the trails of two great branches forming symmetrical coils appears Daniel in the attitude of prayer in the lions' den. The two loaves marked with a cross which are seen at the side near the Prophet's head stand for the food brought to Daniel by Habakkuk, while the dove with the crown in its beak signifies the divine intervention which has closed the lions' mouth.

The *altar* that stands in the centre of the choir has an aperture in front through which may be seen the base within, with spaces for the relics. It is of the 6th century. To the same age belong the porphyry columns of the ancient altar-canopy with their typical capitals two of which show the characteristic Byzantine open-work, while the other are Egyptian-Alexandrian.

The *marble chair* which stands behind is of the Roman period; it has a graceful plant decoration on its sides.

To the 6th century belongs also the marble *pulpit* which rests upon the trunk of a solid column and stands between two of the columns of the nave. It has a curious ovoid shape. It has projecting cornices and is adorned with crosses in very flat relief standing upon globes.

+SCS BALTHASSAR +SCS MELCHIOR +SCS GASPAR

S. Apollinare Nuovo: I Re Magi (VI sec.)

S. Apollinare Nuovo: The three Magi (6th cent.)

Some figures of Prophets and, lower beneath, Theodoric's Palace on the south wall

Some figures of Prophets and, lower beneath, the town of Classe

In spite of the richness of the well balanced marble decoration and the serene composure of the interior, it must be stated that the sacred edifice is famous above all for the superb mosaics which cover the whole length of the walls of the central nave; and to think that originally this mantle of mosaic was evèn more extensive, for it covered also the apse and the inner façade! Moreover, the luminous gleam of the mosaic must have been still further enhanced by the fact that they were mirrored in the marbles which pannelled the side walls, in the stones of the flooring, and in the sunk panels of the roof, which we may reasonably conclude to have been gilded as the church was also described as «in coelo aureo».

The existing mosaics may be divided into three horizontal zones: the first, or upper one, close to the roof (which in its present form with lacunars goes back to the early 17th century), consists of a series of decorative panels alternating with others—26 in all—showing *scenes relating to the miracles and passion of Christ*; the second, which covers the spaces between the windows, shows *male figures* in frontal position; the third, which fills the lowest zone, shows the *procession of Martyrs and Virgins,* and at the end the *Palace of Theodoric* and *the City of Classe* and the groups of *Christ* and the *Madonna flanked by Angels.*

It is not to be thought, however, that all the mosaic decoration belongs to the age of Theodoric. The greater part of it does indeed go back to that time but two large tracts certainly belong to the time of Justinian, and, to be more exact, to the time when Agnellus was Archbishop, for it was he who consecrated the church for Catholic worship. As the author of the «Liber Pontificalis Ecclesiae Ravennatis» tells us, to this period belong the sumptuous mosaics of the two processions—that of the Martyrs and that of the female Saints. The figures of the three Wise Men have also been incontestably shown to be of the same period.

Between the two decorations a period of about forty years elapsed. Though this is but a brief period it is sufficient to reveal

Marble « pluteo » (6th century)

Marble « pluteo » representing Daniel in the lions' den (6th century)

a distinct difference of artistic manner between the two works for the mosaics of Theodoric's time, despite the use of the gold background, present figures with forceful outline, but, especially in the small panels above, they show a certain freedom of movement, together with a spontaneity and animation which are at times truly surprising.

The mosaics of Justinian's time show a composition bound together in rhythms that are repeated with a certain regularity, and cadences which recur at definite intervals.

In the panels showing *scenes of the miracles and passion of the Lord,* which extend, the one along the upper part of the left wall, and the other along the upper part of the right wall, one notes that on the left, the scene generally has few figures and Christ is young and beardless, while on the right the personages are more crowded and Christ is a man of mature age and bearded.

These contrasts indicate not so much a difference in period, as has been thought, but rather a difference of hand; and perhaps we may also say that the artist who designed the cartoons for the panels on the right, had a more outstanding personality, since he reveals higher artistic gifts than the other who planned the decoration on the left.

Both on the right and on the left the scenes relating to the miracles and the passion begin at the further end of the church. The former series starts with the Marriage at Cana (but unfortunately the scene was altered when an unskilful restoration was carried out last century) and ends with the Healing of the paralytic; this has also been restored, for it was damaged by an Austrian bomb which fell upon the church in 1916, but this time the restoration was scrupulously carried out, careful attention being paid to photographs taken previously. All the other panels have come down to us in good state of preservation.

The *Marriage at Cana* is followed by the *Miracle of the Loaves and Fishes*. Next come the *Call of Peter and Andrew*, the *Healing of the Blind Men at Jericho,* and the *Healing of the Wo-*

S. Apollinare Nuovo: Cristo separa le pecore dai capretti - (VI sec.)

S. Apollinare Nuovo: Christ separating the sheep from the goats (6th cent.)

man with the Issue of Blood. The next scenes are: The *Samaritan Woman at the Well,* the *Raising of Lazarus,* the *Pharisee and the Publican at the Temple gate,* and the *Widow offering her Mite.* Lastly, after the scene of the *Separation of the Good from the Bad,* symbolically expressed by two groups, one of sheep, the other of goats, flanked respectively by the Angel of Good, clad in red and the Angel of Evil in blue, come three more miracles: The *Cure at Capernaum of the Paralytic* who is let down through the open roof into the presence of Jesus, the *Healing of the Man possessed of a devil* and the *Cure of the Paralysed Man at Bethesda.*

The scenes of Christ's Passion begin with the Last Supper and end with the Unbelief of St. Thomas. The picture of the *Last Supper* closely resembles in composition an illumination in the famous Greek Evangelistery known as the «Codex Purpureus» which is of the 6th century and is preserved in the Cathedral of Rossano. Then comes *Jesus on the Mount of Olives,* followed by the *Kiss of Judas, Christ before Caiaphas, Jesus tells Peter he will deny him, Peter's Denial.* Next comes the *Remorse of Judas,* and then *Pilate washes his hands,* and *Jesus on his way to Calvary.* Finally one sees the *Three Maries at the Tomb,* the *Walk to Emmaus,* and the *Unbelief of St. Thomas.*

The mosaics between the windows show only male figures—32 in all—in frontal position and holding a scroll or book. They are probably *Prophets.* The design is clear and the modelling fully preserves the sense of volume; all this goes to prove that the mosaicist still adhered to the Hellenistico-Roman artistic tradition.

We cannot say the same for the two admirable *Processions of Martyrs and Virgins,* who, with their slow advance, incessantly repeat the same vertical rhythms, so that their unvarying modulation at once recalls the Byzantine scheme of composition in which one finds over and over again the repetition of the same motif. It is almost like the recitation of so many verses of a Psalm succeeding one another with the same length and the same pauses; it is almost like the monotonous succession of invocations in two long litanies. Indeed one may say at once that these two slow

Processions are nothing but two pictorial litanies, for above the head of every Martyr and every Virgin the name is written.

All the personages are similarly dressed. But the embroidered gold tunics and white veils of the Virgins surpass in richness and splendour the white mantles of the Martyrs led by St. Martin who is the only one to wear a purple cloak.

The Virgins, preceded by the *Three Wise Men* (the upper parts of which have been completely renewed in a recent restoration) move towards the *Madonna with the Child Jesus* on her knee. The Martyrs advance towards *Christ enthroned*, with two Angels on each side. These two groups show such a sense of hieratic dignity that it has been supposed that the artist who planned the composition must have been somewhat influenced by formal oriental schemes.

The representation of the *Palace of Theodoric*, at the beginning of the right wall is curious, not only because some have thought to see here a reproduction in open perspective, of the church prepared for ceremonies (Dyggve), but also because traces are even now visible of a «purge» in the figures of those personages who had originally been represented on the spaces between the columns of the portico. In fact, some hands belonging to these figures can still be seen at the height of about half the length of the columns. Clearly visible too are the semicircular outlines of the heads above the horizontal spears supporting the curtains which Archbishop Agnellus put in place of those figures which very probably representing dignitaries of the Gothic King's Court.

A similar «damnatio memoriae», or «purge» took place also in the case of other figures at one time standing out against the walls of the City of Classe which, with its neighbouring Port, is represented on the opposite wall. There is no doubt that when the basilica was «reconciled» for Catholic worship, the memory of these persons was no longer acceptable.

On the inner façade of the church we now see a rectangular fragment of mosaic showing a *personage with diadem and nimbus,*

« Transenna » - large carved marble panel (6th century)

clad in tunic and mantle. The inscription above names him Justinian, but the inscription was added in a restoration carried out by Kibel in the second half of last century. Considering the difference between this face and that of Justinian in the apse of S. Vitale, some have thought that this may be the mutilated remains of a mosaic with the portrait of King Theodoric (Priess, Lorentz).

THE SO-CALLED PALACE OF THEODORIC

The ancient building commonly called the Palace of Theodoric stands close to the church of S. Apollinare Nuovo. Little more than the façade of it now remains. It certainly is not Theodoric's Palace for it is well known that the King's Palace stood behind the Arian church, and in the early decades of this century Ghirardini unearthed its foundations and reconstructed its plan.

Scholars do not agree in their efforts to fixe the age of this building, or to decide its original purpose. The façade has three distinct parts; the central part has a lofty portal right above which is a large niche in the form of a balcony. The parts which flank the central mass are perfectly symmetrical: below, on each side is an opening with a double arch, and high above it is a blind loggia with three columns resting on a marble bracket. The façade is flanked on both sides by an upright rising almost to the roof below which it forms part of the first arch of the blind loggia.

Some have thought that this building is to be identified as the Guard Room called in ancient times «Calchi», and have assigned it to the end of the 7th, or the beginning of the 8th century (Ricci); others have considered it to be the «Sicreston» or secretarial office of the Exarchs, and have attributed it to the first half of the 8th century (Galassi); others again, and perhaps more reasonably, think that it is the façade of the narthex of the Church of S. Salvatore (Gerola, Verzone); in this case the two small towers with their stairways flanking it at the back would have served merely to give access to the upper galleries or «matroneum» that must have extended above the aisles of the church which (as the excavations have proved) had a central nave, two aisles and a large apse.

However these things may be, it is certain that the architecture of this building, despite the use made of material from earlier edifices, shows such innovations, when compared with other buildings, as to bear witness to the fact that it belongs to a new artistic period.

The so-called Palace of Theodoric

EX-CHURCH OF SANTA CHIARA

(NOW A HOME FOR THE DESTITUTE)

The walls and vaulting of what was once the church of the Convent of St. Clare, was built in 1255 and contains some 14th century frescoes of the Riminese school which are thought (Toesca) to have been painted between 1330 and 1340. They are remarkable also for the fact that they are among the few examples of this artistic manner to be found in Romagna.

In the four triangles of the cross vaulting (which in 1955 were detached and transferred to canvas in order that they might the better be preserved) are the four Evangelists, each with his symbol, and four Doctors of the Church—an Evangelist and a Doctor in each triangle—*St. Jerome and St. Matthew, St. Augustine and St. John, St. Gregory and St. Luke, St. Ambrose and St. Mark.*

On the walls are some scenes from the life of Christ, more or less well preserved: The *Annunciation,* the *Nativity,* the *Adoration of the Magi,* the *Baptism of Christ,* the *Prayer in the Garden* and the *Crucifixion.* There are also some *busts of male and female saints.*

The frescoes of the vaulting are marked by a certain vigour in the rendering of the forms, while those depicting the Annunciation and the Crucifixion are worthy of note particularly for the dramatic animation to be seen in them. Very well balanced and permeated by great loftiness of feeling is the Crucifixion, where the two groups below, the Magdalen and St. John on one side, and the quieter group of the two Maries on the other, face each other at the sides of the crucified Jesus towards whom, on right and left, fly two couples of Angels.

It seems agreed that this cycle of frescoes is the work of more than one master. Some have attributed the whole to Giovanni Baronzio (Van Marle, Berenson), others think that this painter merely presided over the work of the entire decoration (Brach). Again, some are in favour of Pietro and Giuliano da Rimini (Crowe, Cavalcaselle), or of Pietro and Giovanni Baronzio (L. Venturi). Today it seems that the greater part of the decoration may be assigned to Pietro da Rimini who, in certain parts was obliged to call in—as was custom of the time—the collaboration of some assistant who had been trained in his school, which was at the same time not untouched by Sienese influences—especially that of Pietro Lorenzetti (Brandi)—and by the school of Giotto.

SANTA MARIA IN PORTO

(IN THE CITY)

The first stone of this church was laid on Sept. 13th, 1553, and the solemn consecration of the edifice took place on Oct. 8th, 1606. The erection of this monumental basilica was due to the Canons Regular of the Lateran, who had about fifty years earlier abandoned their church of S. Maria in Porto which stood outside the city and which Dante mentions as the

. . . . . . *casa*

di Nostra Donna in sul lito Adriano (Paradise, Canto XXI)

(The house of Our Lady on the Adriatic coast). Despite its isolated position almost three miles from the city, it was razed to the ground in an air raid in 1944 resulting in the irremediable destruction of the fine 14th century frescoes with which Pietro da Rimini (Toesca) had adorned the interior.

The great church which the Canons Regular built in the city, partly with material from the church of S. Lorenzo in Caesarea, shows a white façade in Istrian stone divided into two sections. It is majestic and imposing and is adorned with half-columns and various statues, many of which are the work of Cignaroli; it was finished in the last quarter of the 18th century by the architect Camillo Morigia who, with regard to the lower part, adhered to the lines of an earlier design.

The **interior** (223 ft. by 152 ft.) is in Renaissance style showing Palladian taste; it has a vast and solemn air. The nave is separated from the two aisles by pillars alternating with columns, and crowned at the height of the transept by a lofty cupola (158 ft.).

On the High Altar there is a marble bas-relief of the Virgin at prayer; it is known as the «*Greek Madonna*». This fine figure, which may be of the 11th century (Cecchelli), is of late Byzantine type and was probably brought to Ravenna at the time of the Crusades. According to the legend it flew to the Adriatic shore where it alighted at dawn on April 8th, 1100, preceded by two Angels carrying torches.

Behind the altar is a precious porphyry vase; tradition declares it to be one of the pitchers which, during the marriage feast at Cana, contained the water that the Saviour was to change into wine. It is probably a cinerary urn (Delbrueck).

Around the apse we see a fine set of *Choir stalls* in wood; they were carved between 1576 and 1593 by the hand of a French artist, Mastro Marino.

S. Maria in Porto (in the city) - Marble relief representing the Virgin

S. Maria in Porto (in the city)

The so-called Loggia Lombardesca

CLOISTER OF THE EX-MONASTERY OF S. MARIA IN PORTO AND THE SO-CALLED LOGGIA LOMBARDESCA

Adjoining the Church of S. Maria in Porto is the great **Cloister** which at one time formed part of the Monastery of the Canons Regular of the Lateran. It was begun in the early years of the 16th century by order of Pope Alexander VI, and carried out by Lombard marble-workers. It has a two-storied colonnade, and is impressive for the grace of its architectural lines, and the striking contrast of the white marbles with the plaster of the walls. The regular succession of the arches, though creating a very harmonious rhythm, serves also to impart an increased sense of lightness to the whole.

On the east side the cloister forms an airy loggia—the **Loggia del Giardino** (Garden Loggia)—commonly called the «Loggetta Lombardesca». On the side facing the grassy space in the centre, it is hemmed in by two buildings each having a pointed roof. This beautiful loggia consists of a portico with five arches supported by columns; above it is a second storey resembling that below. The whole is remarkable for the smiling grace of its white stones and the exquisite harmony of its lines.

Theodoric's Mausoleum

THE MAUSOLEUM OF THEODORIC

This mausoleum with its austere and ponderous mass, stands alone in the midst of a group of dark cypress trees, rather less than a mile from the centre of the city, on the furthest verge of the «Campo Coriandro», in a region which the Goths had used as a burying ground, as one concludes from discoveries made on the spot during the last century.

A writer who lived shortly after Theodoric and is known by the name of «Anonimo Valesiano» gives us the important information that the Gothic King «while still living raised to himself a monument built of great squared blocks, to cover which he sought an immense stone».

And in fact this imposing tomb is built of great blocks of Istrian stone, perfectly squared and securely joined together. It consists of two parts, the one above the other. The lower part is decagonal, and on every side there is a wide and deep niche having a round arch formed of large wedge-shaped stones. In the niche facing west there is a door leading into the interior which is in the form of a cross with cross vaulting, and is lighted by six small windows with wide embrasures that enable one to judge of the very considerable thickness of the walls. On the two blocks that jut out from the wall at the further end two shells are carved. From the wall opposite to these, two other masses project: one is still in its rough state, while the other repeats the shell which is, however, merely sketched. It is interesting to notice that the angles of the building are not formed by the conjunction of mutually supporting blocks of stone, but the corner stones were placed in position after having been cut to form the angle.

The upper storey, though somewhat smaller, is also decagonal, but the interior is perfectly circular. On each of the outer walls, except the one with the door, we may see outlines of two rectangular recesses, each surmounted by a lunette in relief. Above this zone the building becomes circular, and on its surface there is a frieze showing a motif suggestive of a pair of pincers.

Upon this circular band rests the massive cover which consists of a huge monolith of Istrian stone measuring about 36 ft. in diameter, and nearly 10 ft. in height. It is believed to weigh about three hundred Italian tons. Along the outer edge of this monolith are carved, at equal distances from one another, twelve «handles», under each of which there is a gap. The usual opinion is that through these holes were passed the ropes by means of which it was possible to carry out the difficult task of raising the mass, with the help, probably of an inclined plane.

One of the problems which have most wearied scholars is that which relates to the original appearance of the upper storey, and of the manner in which the lower and the upper parts were connected.

Some have thought that all round the upper part there was a sort of covered gallery supported by slender columns (Vandelli, Ginanni); another has thought that at the sides of the decagon there were two arched niches jutting outward and supported by slender columns (Schulz); again, it has been suggested that originally all the side were quite smooth, and that it was only later that the rectangular recesses and lunettes were added (Durm); it has also been maintained that the original plan was to carry the decagonal form up to and including the roof (Fiechter) and that it was only the possibility of making use of a great monolith which caused the project to be modified (Cecchelli). Finally the theory has been advanced—and it seems the most probable—that on each face of the decagon there was a decoration of simple pensile arches (Ricci, Guberti) which some consider was never completed (Haupt, Gerola).

With regard to the heterogeneous circular cap of the mausoleum set upon a decagonal body, Ferry has recently made some remarkable observations, and has given a singular explanation for various decorative and architectural features to which earlier scholars had not paid very much attention. Thus, Ferri thought that the upper part of the monument—contrarily to the laws of functionality in the Roman architectural tradition—was made circular, because Theodoric desired that his tomb should have, at least in the upper part, the form of the tents in use among his ancestors. It is for this reason that Ferri sees in the frieze with its pincers-like design, not merely an ornamental element typical of northern art, but the translation into stone of a functional object of metal, i.e. the four hooks moving in opposite directions united with a pivot so as to form a cross; these hooks so operated as to facilitate the passage into and out of the tent that was made up of several widths of canvas; these, in order the better to be seen, have not been shown hanging straight down as they would normally appear, but with a rotation of 90 degrees.

Ferri found support for this brilliant theory of his in the presence of other elements which, now translated into stone, no longer have the functional character which was originally theirs. For example, he considers that the twelve modillions upon the edge of the cap—on the outer faces of which are carved the names of the four Evangelists and eight of the Apostles—were not so planned as to supply a means of raising the enormous monolith, but in order to reproduce the appearance of the top of a tent supported upon strong poles, which, radiating from the centre, reached the circumference and then projected from it each forming a hook.

Proceeding still further along these lines, Ferri sees in the

Theodoric's portrait on the gold medallion coming from Senigallia, now in the National Roman Museum

cross painted upon the summit of the ceiling of the enormous cap, a motif, well suited certainly to a sepulchral chamber, but a structure corresponding to the «decussatio viminea» of the Asiatic tents, in which two poles laid at right angles one to another were crossed by a circular opening to let out the smoke; this opening was closed during the night and in wet weather by a large disc, and this has been reproduced on the exterior of the mausoleum in the great central disc which is about 12 ft. in diameter, and overlaps the rest by about four inches.

These twelve modillions could certainly never have supported statues, as has been thought (Fabbri), for on their upper part they are not level, but for some scholars they have recalled «materially the armed head of a warrior, and symbolically the savage might of war» (Guberti).

On entering the upper storey of the monument, one sees in the centre a large porphyry coffin; it must at one time have contained the Gothic King's remains which were later lost. Then, on gazing up from the inside at the great monolith, one is clearly able to see on one side a crack reaching almost to the top. It is exceedingly likely that it was caused by a jolt when the stone was being lifted into place, but a legend handed down in Ravenna from generation to generation offers another explanation. It is said among the people that the crack was caused when a lightning struck the building, on the very day when Theodoric, whose death by lightning had been foretold to him, had taken refuge there during a terrible storm. But in spite of this the lightning, cleaving its way through the mighty stone, struck the Arian King and reduced his body to ashes.

S. Apollinare in Classe

+SANCTVS
APOLENARIS

S. Apollinare in Classe: Mosaici dell'abside e dell'arco trionfale

Basilica of St. Apollinare in Classe: interior

SANT'APOLLINARE IN CLASSE

Bishop Maximian, whose fortunate lot it had been to consecrate S. Vitale, shortly afterwards—on May 9th, 549—also consecrated the large imposing basilica of S. Apollinare in Classe. The name «in Classe» derives from the neighbouring «oppidum Classis», the town which sprang up in defence of the famous Port founded by Augustus. And it was to the inhabitants of this «castrum» or fort, who were mainly merchants and seamen, that S. Apollinaris, the first Bishop of Ravenna, brought the good tidings of the new Faith, the comforting words of the Gospel. We do not know exactly when he lived: it is hardly likely that we must go back so far as the age of the Apostles, as is suggested in the «Passio S. Apollinaris», a legendary narrative drawn up probably at the end of the 5th or at the beginning of the 6th century (Mazzotti). The desire to go back to this ancient time shows that the hagiographer, while wishing to ennoble the figure of the first Bishop, tried at the same time to shed further glory upon the origin of the church of his city.

Very soon cemeteries arose around the town of Classe, and these were in part used by the Christians, as can be proved from the discovery there of various funerary inscriptions. Beside, rather than upon, one of these burying grounds, as De Rossi has thought, Bishop Ursicinus, in the second quarter of the 6th century, built the magnificent church of Classe which now stands almost alone (at least for the present) in the midst of the country, whilst behind it, towards the sea, stretches the dark green of that vast pine wood «spessa e viva» (thick and living) of which Dante and Byron sang.

The Church is about four miles from the centre of Ravenna, and is now far from the sea which was at one time very near it. It can be seen from afar, not so much by reason of its imposing mass, as for the tall and massive **Campanile** (123 ft. high), belonging perhaps to the end of the 10th century, which is rendered more slender and graceful in appearance by the ascending series of windows—the lowest with a single opening («monofore»), the next above with two openings («bifore»), and the third with three («trifore»). In these latter there are white columns with characteristic crutch-shaped capitals.

Julianus Argentarius, who financed the construction of S. Vitale, undertook the considerable task of building this church too, and it is for that reason that one sees here the long thin red bricks which are to be seen in all Julianus's other edifices.

This church, which has the usual basilican form, at first had an atrium in front of it, as is proved by the fact that some remains of it were discovered last century. To the central block of the façade, flanked on their side by two smooth uprights, is added the narthex which has on its left a high quadrangular building which has been a great deal restored. There must also have been a similar structure on the right, for it has been possible to trace its foundations.

A rhythmical design of blind arches supported by uprights enlivens the side walls of the exterior, in which there are numerous wide windows. The apse, semicircular inside, is polygonal outside. Beside the apse stand the two square chapels known as the «prothesis» and the «diaconicon», each of which has a small pentagonal apse.

The **interior** (182 ft. by 99 ft.) is spacious and solemn, and is impressive especially for the great width of the central nave, which is flanked by two rows of magnificent marble columns

S. Apollinare in Classe - Interior

from the workshops of Proconnesos. They are marked by horizontal veining, are raised upon square bases and are surmounted by capitals carved with leaves that seem blown out by the wind. Above the capitals are «pulvini». The whole of this material shows the most homogeneous uniformity of style and measurement, so that there is no doubt that it was expressly ordered for the erection of this church.

The side walls, in each of which there were originally three doors, are now a bare and unadorned expanse of brick, but once they were covered with panels of polished marble, for Andrea-Agnello writes in his «Liber Pontificalis Ecclesiae Ravennatis», that no church in Italy was so rich in valuable stones—«in lapidibus preciosis»—. These marbles were in great part carried away in the first half of the 15th century when Sigismondo Pandolfo Malatesta asked for and obtained them to decorate the church at Rimini which took its name from him.

The choir of the church is now raised well above the level of the nave: this is due to the addition below it of the crypt, which is semicircular in form with a central corridor. Some critics think it was built in the 7th century (Grabar), according to others (Mazzotti) towards the end of the 9th, while yet others (Ricci) attribute it to the second half of the 12th. In any case it is certain that when the basilica was built, instead of the raised choir, there was the «bema», or enclosure reserved for the clergy; this extended towards the centre of the edifice as far as the two third columns from the further end. In fact, its foundations—upon which must have rested the carved sections and small marble pilasters for the parapet surrounding it—were brought to light in 1953 about one foot below the level of the present flooring, as the result of certain careful investigations.

Of the ancient mosaic pavement which must have covered the whole of this vast building like an immense carpet, a few remains have been found at the end of the left aisle, and at the beginning of the right. Here an expanse of mosaic, showing geometrical designs, preserves an inscription recording that a great part of this work was done at her personal expense by a certain

The mosaic decoration of the apse and the choir arch.

lady «Gaudentia», and a certain «Felix», together with other benefactors. Another fragment of mosaic, discovered in 1953 below the flooring of the central nave, has been affixed to the right wall of the church.

But the thing which most arrests the attention of the visitor as he enters the church of S. Apollinare in Classe, is without doubt the sumptuous many-coloured mantle of mosaic which covers the **choir arch** and the **semidome of the apse.**

Not all this mosaic, however, belongs to the same period. The upper part of the arch would seem to go back, according to some scholars (Toesca) to the 7th century, but according to others (Galassi) it is to be attributed to the 9th. In the upper part, which stretches horizontally over the whole width above the arch, is a figure of *Christ* with wide open eyes and wrinkled brow, within a medallion. Beside him, in the midst of a sea of stylised clouds, are the *winged symbols of the Evangelists*, the Eagle, the Man, the Lion and the Bull; in the last figure it is to be noticed that the head is drawn strictly in profile but the nostrils appear to be in a perfectly frontal position. The zone below these figures shows on the extreme right and left the two symbolical *cities of Jerusalem and Bethlehem*, their walls adorned with precious stones. From their gates issue *twelve lambs*, six on each side, which advance upwards towards the Christ in the medallion above; we have here undoubtedly a symbolic representation of the twelve Apostles.

In the narrow spaces beside the arch two palm trees stand out on a dark blue background. This part of the mosaic is to be assigned to the 6th century, as are also the figures below representing the *Archangels Gabriel and Michael*, who, like celestial warriors, carry the «labarum» or banner bearing the praise of the Thrice Holy God. Lower still we see the figures belonging to the 12th century (Toesca) of *St. Matthew* and, perhaps, *St. Luke.*

The entire decoration of the dome of the apse is to be attributed to about the middle of the 6th century. The composition, based on the agreement of colours few but bright, falls naturally into two parts. Above, upon a sky of gold streaked by many small

S. Apollinare in Classe - St. Apollinaris

clouds, stands a great jewelled disc which contains a cross studded with many precious stones; this, in its turn, at the point where the arms cross, bears within a circle the head of Christ. The upper part of the cross is surmounted by the Greek word ΙΧΘΥC; the word means «fish» and the letters of the Greek word stand for the initial letters of «Jesus Christ Son of God Saviour». Beneath the cross we read the words: «Salus Mundi» i.e. Salvation of the World.

This great medallion is flanked by the figures of *Moses* and *Elijah* emerging from the clouds. Their presence clearly proves that the artist is alluding to the Transfiguration of Christ on Mt. Tabor, which was witnessed by the Apostles Peter, James and John, whom we must recognize as being represented symbolically by the *three white lambs* which stand below but raise their heads towards the jewelled cross.

Lower down the zone widens out into a green flowery valley, varied by the emergence of small dark rocks bordered with white, and enlivened by a luxuriant growth of grass, bushes and other plants among which we may see the pine—the tree which is still today especially characteristic of the countryside around Ravenna. In the centre of this scene, which has a soft shade of green for background, stands the tall, solemn imposing figure of *St. Apollinaris* wearing, over his white alb, the chasuble adorned with many golden bees—the symbol of eloquence. The first Bishop of Ravenna is in the attitude of an «orans» i.e. he is pictured at the moment of uttering his prayers that God will grant his heavenly grace to the faithful entrusted to his care who are here seen as *twelve lambs* that surround him. It is for this reason that the composition might almost be said to be inspired by the last words of the sermon which St. Peter Chrysologus preached in honour of St. Apollinaris: «Ecce vivit, ecce ut bonus Pastor suo medio assistit in grege» (Behold he lives, behold how the good Shepherd stands in the midst of his flock).

The figures of the Bishops Severus, Ecclesius, Ursus and Ursicinus clad in their sacred vestments, which are seen in the

S. Apollinare in Classe: Il Vescovo Ecclesius

S. Apollinare in Classe: Bishop Ecclesius

The sarcophagus of Bishop Theodorus in the right aisle

The marble canopy

spaces between the windows, are contemporary with the building of the church.

The two panels seen at the side of the apse are a little more than a century later: in the right we see the *Sacrifices of Abel, Abraham and Melchizedek* where the composition is not devoid of balance, but the colours are weak and undecided. On the left are the *Emperor Constantine IV Pogonatus* (*the bearded*) *with his brothers Heraclius and Tiberius in the act of handing the rescript of «Privileges» to Reparatus, the delegate of Archbishop Maurus.* The work reechoes the one seen on the panels of the apse of S. Vitale, but during the course of centuries, it has undergone various alterations, so that today we see it almost all restored in tempera to imitate mosaic.

There are some important **sarcophagi** lining the side walls of the church. They belong to the 5th, 6th, 7th and 8th centuries, and by taking them in turn one can gain an idea of the development of sculpture throughout this period. One notices how, from the sculptured figures of the Apostles which in the art of Ravenna are typical of the 5th century one passes in the next century and those that follow, to representations in which their symbolical and decorative character is increased by the lack of modelling, and indeed by a very marked flatness.

Also worthy of note is the *marble canopy* over the altar at the further end of the left aisle; from the inscription around the upper border we learn that it was erected at the beginning of the 9th century in honour of the third Bishop of Ravenna St. Eleucadius. Beneath the canopy, and affixed to the wall, are two small marble panels showing the *Annunciation*; in one the Angel advances with his staff and stretching out his hand as he speaks; in the other the Virgin is seen seated in the act of spinning purple thread. These two small panels are to be assigned, not so much to the 7th century as some have said (Gerspach), as to the 10th.

CONTENTS

Finito di stampare il 10 marzo 1969
per conto delle Ed. A. Longo - Ravenna
dalla tipo-lito Stimmatini - Verona